Mastering Life

MW00980511

Also by Dr. Kollar

Solution-Focused Pastoral Counseling

Mastering Life

Getting with God's
Program
for Your Future

Charles Allen Kollar

ZondervanPublishingHouse
Grand Rapids, Michigan

A Division of HarperCollinsPublishers

Mastering Life
Copyright © 1999 by Charles A. Kollar

Requests for information should be addressed to:

📖 ZondervanPublishingHouse
Grand Rapids, Michigan 49530

Library of Congress Cataloging-in-Publication Data

Kollar, Charles Allen, 1953–
    Mastering life : getting with God's program for your future / Charles Allen
Kollar.
       p.   cm.
    Includes bibliographical references and index.
    ISBN 0-310-22775-5 (softcover: alk. paper)
    1. Christian life. 2. Problem solving—Religious aspects—Christianity. I. Title.
BV4501.2.K59 1999
248.4—dc21
                                      99-29664
                                          CIP

All Scripture quotations, unless otherwise indicated, are taken from the *Holy Bible: New
International Version®*. NIV®. Copyright © 1973, 1978, 1984 by International Bible
Society. Used by permission of Zondervan Publishing House. All rights reserved.

All rights reserved. No part of this publication may be reproduced, stored in a retrieval
system, or transmitted in any form or by any means—electronic, mechanical, photocopy,
recording, or any other—except for brief quotations in printed reviews, without the
prior permission of the publisher.

The identities of those who have come to the author for counseling have been carefully
disguised in accordance with professional standards of confidentiality and in keeping
with their rights to privileged communication. All names and identifying background
information have been changed.

Interior design by Sherri L. Hoffman

Printed in the United States of America

---

99 00 01 02 03 04 05 /❖ DC/ 10 9 8 7 6 5 4 3 2 1

To Frank and Elisabeth

Contents

Special Thanks

To the Master of Life. Thank You for giving to me a small fragment of Your infinite knowledge.

To my family. Thank you, Dawn, for your consistent love and support. Nathan, Joshua, and Heather—you have grown into loving young adults right before my eyes.

To Kevin Kollar. Thank you for reading the initial manuscript and offering your support and valuable suggestions.

To my editors at Zondervan, Jim Ruark and Mary McNeil. Thanks for offering your words of encouragement and for putting up with my many changes to the manuscript. Change is inevitable.

Preface

Every time you make a choice you are turning the central part of you, the part that chooses, into something a little different than it was before. And taking your life as a whole, with all your innumerable choices, you are slowly turning this central thing either into a Heavenly creature or into a hellish creature.

C. S. Lewis

This book is not only a book to read, it is a book to use. Although there are numerous illustrations regarding the principles presented, it is not my intention to tell you how to live your life. Rather, I assume that God is actively at work within you. As His intention unfolds and you deliberately come into agreement with it, life will teach you what you need to know. Yet, for this to happen you must become increasingly aware of your choices as they are being made. These choices are the result of what you truly believe—not what you "say" you believe. Your character *is* being formed by each choice. Good choices bring forth a healthy character, which in turn brings out the best of your unique, God-given personality. Of course, bad choices result in an untrustworthy character, bringing out the worst aspects of your personality. I do not believe there is any way around this.

Thus, each chapter of this book introduces essential skills needed to master life. Solution-focused living is the key to effective problem-resolution skills. Such skills increase your personal competence and will help you more confidently solve problems successfully in the days and years ahead.

At the end of each chapter are action steps, which are built on key concepts from the chapter. (You may find it helpful to keep a notebook or journal to track your progress through the action steps.) Although this book can help you to solve problems, it cannot solve them for you. That would be too easy! Ultimately, lasting change remains your responsibility. The greater your willingness and commitment to the process of your own growth, the greater your level of accomplishment. Remember, too, the Holy Spirit, who is a master counselor, has already planned for your success.

Introduction

When first considering the title *Mastering Life,* I felt that it was overstated—pretentious even. Would it be possible to deliver on such a grand theme? Indeed, could a book written by any author carry out such an ambitious goal? That, of course, is the point. Such a book does not exist and will not exist. Even the Bible does not make such a claim. What it does present to those who embrace it with an open heart, is a record of the Creator of the universe breaking into human history. This record, accurately recorded, included flawed and imperfect humanity wrestling with what this message might mean.

Today, as its pages are opened, our thoughts are transported into possibilities that would have moments earlier seemed distant and unattainable. Then, as each one presses toward these possibilities with a tenacious faith, the experience of God touches our hearts at a deeply personal level. It is this encounter that transforms daily experiences—enduing them with far-reaching implications and practical life-changing realities.

These implications and life-changing realities need to be clearly identified as each person walks the walk of faith. It is in the *doing* that the mastering of life takes place. In it we discover that, even when alternating between days of dreary sameness, moments of terrifying violence, and those blessed times of gentleness and safety, the experience of life is always true. And this primary reality is at the heart of all that is. Life is, and always has been, an education. When we fail to recognize the hand of the Master, and the teaching of the Spirit, we miss the essential life-transforming nature of each moment's lesson. But for those with eyes to see and ears to hear, all of life comes alive with meaning. Life *is* the miracle—all the miracle any of us needs to be fully formed by the Spirit into sons and daughters of God.

As such, we are uniquely made in God's image. Coming into agreement with His intention for our lives—we cannot fail! That's right. God has placed us on this earth to succeed. The twists, turns, ups, and downs of this ride we call life are all essential. God has factored each into His overall intention for our lives. As you read this book, it is my hope that you will come to know and trust the true Master of Life as the One who created and put into place this journey for your benefit. I believe we cannot help but become what God wants us to become. Abundant life is not a distant hope but a present reality.

As a rising tide lifts all the ships in the harbor, so also an increased level of personal competency, that is, mastering the skill of living, will benefit every other area of life. The skill is in mastering life for ourselves—not fearing the sudden twists and turns. Again, failure is not an option. Our every perceived failure has been accounted for. God has already woven every trauma, tragedy, disappointment, and discouragement into the fabric of each life.

So how do we begin? *Mastering Life* presents a natural and spontaneous view of Christian growth. It also gives a specific procedure for encouraging that growth—in agreement with our primary counselor, God's Holy Spirit. As you continue to read, you will discover that God has given each of us an imagination as our fundamental resource. You will learn how to use it to create a new picture of life by unlocking a vision without the everyday problems, deliberately creating a new vision of your future, and getting on track toward living that vision today. You will learn how to trust in God's intention and purpose during experiences that would once have caused great distress. Although this initially seems to be a mystery, Christ is being formed in you. You are developing the mind of Christ, the ability to see options and possibilities in the midst of the storm. But it takes the proper use of your God-given imagination.

Then you will be happy to learn that you are the expert on your life, and you can learn how to intentionally come into agreement with the Master. This acceptance of personal responsibility will put you into the very heart of the transforming design of the Holy Spirit. You can create a vision of your future where you are taking greater action to solve your own problems. The goal will be to initiate a pattern for future success—rather than focusing on past failures. Vague goals are hard to visualize and even harder to accomplish. Specific goals will provide for you a sense of how you will know when you are on track.

Yet, from time to time you will get stuck. You will learn that your problems need not represent symptoms of deeper dysfunctions. Rather, they more often represent the confines of your present perceptions. You will learn about the honest limitations of your brain's neural pathways and the incredible truth that you are created to have access into God's thought patterns—the mind of Christ. Then, after you have been told again and again by the world that change is difficult—or even impossible—you will come to realize that change is actually inevitable. You can learn to seize the opportunity to change in a way that leads toward new solutions rather than toward a continuation of old or present problems. As you see this, you will discover that nothing is quite so ordinary and obvious as it first appears. Indeed, God is found in the obvious and the ordinary. You are being rewritten by His love.

We will also look together at the complexity of the problems in our lives. Although problems are often complex, solutions need not be. You will learn to listen and focus more on God's intention rather than on the rattles and bumps of the ride. That is, you will learn to stop doing what is *not* working and start doing more of what *is* working. Shifting your perspective in this way will help you discover how good or better things happen, how you can continue to have these good things happen, and how to build on them. Your strengths will be utilized to encourage these "better" times to happen more often.

Most important, you will be reminded again and again that God has touched your life. As you come into agreement with what God is already doing, His intention becomes the key to your life. In becoming aware of and in agreement with His intention, you will begin to recognize His writing, grace, and design—which is infinitely greater than anything you now perceive. Therefore, you will learn to "critique" life's experiences in light of what you are investigating regarding God's intention.

In this way, as you get deliberately involved in the development of your own life, you will begin to see the change. You cannot help but grow in Christ if you will seriously pay attention. You need to be willing to learn, to see what God is doing each day, to be trained by Him, and to apply these lessons in your various roles and responsibilities. Then, as you visualize your life without the dominance of present and past problems, you develop a new perception; you see yourself doing something different—you are seeing your life without the problem. With this new perspective you will discover that the problems that are now holding you back were not always present—nor are they always happening now. Finding these *exceptions* to your problems will help reveal your strengths and capabilities—and also reveal what to do next.

Finally, as you start to behave in ways that actually work, you will begin to do more of the same on purpose—observing what is working and doing it deliberately. Learning how to slow down your reactive impulse and becoming more purposeful in your approach to life and decision making. Your actions will more often invite cooperation from others rather than defensiveness as you recognize the problem as the problem, not any individual—including yourself. Your responsibility is to remove the barriers to God's purposes and intentions. You will learn to create a loving environment where you and your family can become healthy and feel loved. Your own personal health will then open the door to new possibilities to grow and be built up in love.

Throughout this book, life is viewed as the ultimate adventure. This is not to imply that life is safe. It most certainly is not. Life is real. It is, at its essence, a potentially terrifying experience. Indeed, something has gone terribly wrong. We live in a world of broken people. So many are not even able to command obedience from their own thoughts and emotions. Yet, this essential wrongness and brokenness has been factored into the perfection of each individual that places himself or herself into the hands of the Creator. God has not been surprised by the damage inflicted on His world. Even though the journey of life will take everything we have to complete successfully, God has clearly pointed the way.

Although each life impacts so many others, at its core, life is a deeply personal experience, personally designed by God for each individual. No one can fathom the depth or uniqueness of your life. Nothing can compare to the personal training that God's Spirit has already begun within you. Not one moment or experience will be wasted. Most important, you have nothing to fear. So get ready. He longs to give to each of us who will come to Him in simple faith and with a humble spirit, the keys to mastering life.

part one

Getting with God's Program for Your Future

chapter one

Mind Your Imagination

Man's mind, once stretched by a new idea, never regains its original dimension.

OLIVER WENDELL HOLMES

Imagination is more important than knowledge.

ALBERT EINSTEIN

I recall the excitement I felt on the day my parents and I went to see the parade. It was July 4, 1962, and I was nine years old. So many floats and magnificent marching bands—the memory still shines so brightly. What excitement! My two older brothers were there, marching in the school band. The bright colors of the uniforms, the reflection of the summer sun flashing off each instrument ... People were cheering. Little American flags seemed to be waving everywhere I looked. It was exhilarating.

Then it happened. The crowd surged forward, all wanting to see their sons, daughters, brothers, and sisters in the band. Being a small fellow, I was soon up to my eyes in hips, legs, and purses. I was stuck, no way out—and I could hear my brothers' marching band almost directly in front of me. I felt so helpless. I could not see a thing, and soon it would be too late. My feeling of excitement quickly evaporated, turning to frustration, and from frustration to fear. Tears were rolling down my face. I felt trapped.

Without warning, two strong hands gripped my waist from behind. In a flash I was lifted up on my father's shoulders. What a transformation! In a single moment my emotions changed from tears and frustration to joy and elation. I could see everything, the floats and clowns that had passed by, and now, finally, my brothers' band with its trumpets gleaming and its drums tapping out the rhythm.

Looking back at that day, I ask myself—what really happened? What changed? The parade was the same. The crowd was still surging around me. Everything was the same. No, that is not completely true. One thing had changed—my perspective. While on the ground, I was cut off from what I most wanted to see. My goal was blocked! On my father's shoulders I could see it all.

So it is with the problems we face today. Together they are often overwhelming, crowding us in. Sometimes it seems that they could almost block out the sun—or all that we most wish for. Yet, we receive a new perspective when our Father in heaven lifts us up on His shoulders. Though the problem may still exist, He gives us new options, a new way of looking at the situation. With a new vision comes the opportunity to act in a new way. Fear gives way to hope, despair gives way to faith, and discouragement gives way to joy. It can all happen so quickly.

With a new vision comes the opportunity to act in a new way.

Sometimes we get *stuck* in the midst of our problems. Something limits our ability to discover these new possibilities and options. In the midst of a crisis, or when inundated with the stresses of daily living, we can develop an "emotional myopia."

WHAT IS EMOTIONAL MYOPIA?

Myopia is a disease of the eye that results in a diminished capacity to see peripherally, that is, on the outer edge of our field of vision. In time the one afflicted with this illness sees only what is directly in front of him, and that portion of sight decreases as well—often leading to blindness. So also, we can fail to "see" that which is beyond our range of vision. All we see in front of us is the problem. We live with it all day, and it is still before our eyes when we try to sleep at night. In the morning it crowds back into our thoughts unbidden. We stew and mull and think and pray until one day we realize that we are accomplishing nothing, that all our stewing has gotten us no closer to a solution.

When teaching about the kingdom of God, Jesus often commented on how hard it is to see beyond an established way of thinking. His words were unlike anything the crowds had ever heard. His perceptions did not fit their expectations. Of those who saw His miracles, some He declared "blind" (Matt. 23:26). Others heard each word, yet did not "hear." Of such Jesus said,

> If we keep doing what we have always been doing, we will keep getting what we have always been getting.

"Therefore I speak to them in parables, because seeing they do not see, and hearing they do not hear, nor do they understand" (Matt. 13:13 NKJV). We all have self-imposed rules and regulations that influence our way of thinking. These filter all incoming information—and filter out whatever does not make sense.

As important as this ability may be, it can also result in our becoming blind and deaf to *creative solutions*. We allow our fixed ways of thinking to have the power to keep us from hearing and seeing what *could* happen. When it comes to our problems one thing is clear . . . if we keep doing what we have always been doing, we will keep getting what we have always been getting. This results in numerous personal limitations, often a form of intellectual and emotional myopia.

THE STORY OF THE SWISS WATCHMAKERS

In my book *Solution-Focused Pastoral Counseling* I shared a story I had heard regarding the devastating lesson Swiss watch manufacturers learned earlier this century. Just thirty years ago Swiss watches were the standard for excellence throughout the world. The Swiss made nearly eighty percent of all watches sold.

> Do not be blinded by past victories and glories, even when they are the result of God's manifested power and deliverance.

Today, Swiss watchmakers make less than ten percent. Thousands of expert artisans lost their jobs. How did this happen?

It was a Swiss technician who created the quartz watch. He had managed to reach beyond the belief that watches must have gears and springs. His superiors, on the other hand, were still constrained by their previous beliefs and traditions. They proclaimed that watches must have gears and springs. Indeed, so sure were they of their convictions that they did not bother to protect their ownership of the quartz design. They were blinded by their previous success. Some years later the watch was displayed at a world's fair. Representatives from two young companies were very interested in it. One representative was from Seiko and the other from Texas Instruments. The rest is history.

The Old Testament prophet Isaiah presents a similar "blindness."

FORGET THE RED SEA

More than two millennia ago Isaiah saw this potential hazard. It plagued God's people then as it does today. He cried out to them the words of God: "Forget the former things; do not dwell on the past. See, I am doing a new thing! Now it springs up; do you not perceive it? I am making a way in the desert and streams in the wasteland" (Isa. 43:18–19). What was he telling them to forget? He was teaching them to not be blinded by past victories and glories—even when these were the result of God's manifested power and deliverance. Listen to what the prophet had said in the previous three verses: "I am the LORD, your Holy One, Israel's Creator, your King. This is what the LORD says—he who made a way through the sea, a path through the mighty waters, who drew out the chariots and horses, the army and reinforcements together, and they lay there, never to rise again, extinguished, snuffed out like a wick" (vv. 15–17).

What is Isaiah referring to? Incredibly, it was the miraculous parting of the Red Sea—the one event that galvanized the young nation of Israel. It was an astonishing display of raw power by an omnipotent Creator. Now this same Creator is saying in essence, "Get over it! I am doing something new!" God's people had been blinded by their previous success. Having become satisfied and complacent in their glorious history, they could not see that God was about to do something new. In this case God ultimately defeats the nation of Babylon and brings the Israelites back to their homeland, a victory that will outshine the many wonders of Israel's history.

For Israel then, and the church today, Isaiah reveals a principle that we often fail to recognize. That is, in our lives we get stuck when we become complacent or satisfied with how we have dealt with problems in the past. The Holy Spirit is using this roller coaster we call life to teach us a different lesson—but we do not see or hear what it is.

THE WISE CHINESE FARMER

The story is told of a wise old farmer in China many years ago. He lived a humble life—a small plot of land, one son, an old plow horse, and a plow. He and his son worked long hours plowing the land in order to feed themselves and offer to others what little they had left over. He had a generous spirit and the wisdom that often comes to those who have been trained by life's experiences.

Early one morning, as he was preparing to begin the work of the day, he discovered that his plow horse had run away during the night. This was devastating news. It meant that he and his son would have to pull the heavy plow through the rocky soil themselves. When word got out, the other nearby farmers, and even some of the local villagers, came by to console the old man. "What bad luck," they exclaimed. The old man simply replied, "Good luck ... bad luck ... who knows?"

The following day the old plow horse returned home, bringing with him a herd of wild horses. Immediately, the old gentleman's fortunes had changed. All the farmers and villagers returned, this time to congratulate him on his good luck. The old man simply replied, "Good luck ... bad luck ... who knows?"

The next day, while attempting to tame the wild horses, the old man's son was thrown from a horse—breaking his leg. The local farmers and villagers returned once again to console the old man. "Now you will have to work twice as hard," they exclaimed. "What bad luck!" Looking at his friends and neighbors he simply replied, "Good luck ... bad luck ... who knows?"

Later that same week the emperor's army came marching through the village and farms conscripting all able-bodied young men to fight in the emperor's army. All the young men of the village, and even those throughout the surrounding countryside, were taken. None were spared, except one—the old farmer's son. He was allowed to remain due to his broken leg. Again, all the local farmers and villagers came to visit the old man and congratulate him on his good fortune. "What good luck you have," they cried out. Pausing to consider his words the old farmer replied knowingly, "Good luck . . . bad luck . . . who knows?"

Now tell me, was this good luck or bad luck? . . . Who knows?

Although as Christians we do not believe in concepts such as luck or fortune, the old man's wisdom lies in his far-reaching vision. Having learned that one event interacts with another—often in ways quite unexpected—he remained open to change. He expected the unexpected, and thus he was prepared for any eventuality. He had managed to reach beyond the belief that one event leads inexorably to the next. He had learned that what may seem good in the present may not bring forth the results that were so eagerly anticipated. He also knew that what seemed to be a problem, sometimes one of even tragic proportions, might lead to unanticipated gains.

How much more is this true for those who place their faith in an all-knowing and loving heavenly Father. For this reason, the apostle Paul was able to exclaim with such confidence that "in all things God works for the good of those who love him, who have been called according to his purpose" (Rom. 8:28). Paul believed that God saw his whole life—past, present, and future—and that His *intention* for him was good. Even during Paul's darkest moments, this belief anchored his mind in God's eternal plan.

> **What seems to be a problem, sometimes one of even tragic proportions, may lead to unanticipated gains.**

So also, as you place your faith in His Son, Jesus Christ, you will begin to realize that your heavenly Father is "causing" all things to work together for your good. As you enter into a more personal relationship with God and trust in His purpose, your perspective grows. You can now begin to trust in God's intention and purpose during experiences that would once have caused great distress. This appears to us as a great mystery, but Christ is being "formed in you," and you are developing the "mind of Christ," the ability to see options and possibilities in the midst of the storm. To do this takes the proper use of your God-given imagination.

BACK FROM THE FUTURE

After all, why did God give us an imagination? Too often it is used for all the wrong reasons. Yet, with a healthy one, it is also possible to see life from a whole new perspective. I recall a time a few years ago when my imagination presented me with possibilities that I could not have come by any other way. It occurred at a Little League baseball game. I was the coach for our church team. My oldest son, Nathan, was twelve years old at the time. My son Joshua was ten, and my daughter Heather was eight. The boys were on one team and Heather was playing nearby on another. The fields were back-to-back, so I could view both games, even though I was coaching only my sons' team. Suddenly, I had a truly extraordinary notion that I was actually "back in time" watching *my now grown sons and daughter* playing as children. It was as if I were an elderly man, and God had allowed me to pick one day to go back and relive. Evidently, I had picked *this* day, and there were my children, little again.

What a thrill it was to see them, not only to watch from a distance, but also to interact and to touch their lives once more. The uniforms were such a bright red, the sky a peaceful blue. The sun was brightly shining on my children as they took the field, rounded the bases, pounded their gloves, kicked at the dirt, and swung the bat. I received this insight as a gift from the Lord. I realized at that moment, if given the chance to live life over again, there would be so many things I would do to let them know how special they were to me. Yet, here I was. It was still today, and the opportunity had not been forever lost. Oh, how I loved them with renewed enthusiasm. To see them, to touch them. For me, this day took on even greater meaning and joy.

Can you imagine yourself to be quite elderly, in the winter of your life, children grown and gone? Or, perhaps your present life is over altogether, and God has allowed you the opportunity to go back and be with loved ones again—for just one day. What will that day be like for you? *You can live that day today.* "This is the day that the Lord has made. . . ."

IMAGINATION

Consider the creative approach practiced by the imagineers of Walt Disney Imagineering (WDI). For years this company has used a concept called *imagineering* to assist them in creating theme parks and the attractions inside those parks. They carefully visualize their desired outcome: a perfect attraction. We could view this as a "problem-free" attraction. When the imagineers are creating this perfect attraction, they must think through the entire project from beginning to end, seeking at every stage to create something new, something better. We can use this concept of imagineering to break through spiritual myopia—"established" theories and entrenched beliefs.

> When you visualize what you will be doing or saying before acting, you become solution-focused rather than problem-focused.

Just like the Disney imagineers, your desired outcome needs to guide your actions. When you visualize what you will be doing or saying before acting, you become solution-focused rather than problem-focused. This will affect how you think about people, change how you talk to yourself, and improve how you create solutions. What we all need, as followers of Jesus Christ, is some personal imagineering—learning how to get on track with our personal goals and relationships.

Remember, life is a challenge. It is serious business and responsibility. Yet, in the heart of your often hectic, sometimes tedious, experience of life, you are to have a deliberate awareness of being in the heart of God's intention. You can have spontaneous joy, incomprehensible peace, and adventurous excitement in the midst of absolute seriousness. My hope is that you will be encouraged to see beyond your problem, to deliberately create a new vision for your future, and to get on track toward living your vision today.

Key Points and Action Steps for Personal Application

KEY CONCEPT 1

A new vision brings an opportunity to act in a new way. Over the years you have developed self-imposed rules and regulations that have influenced your way of thinking. Remember, if you keep doing what you have always been doing, you will keep getting what you have always been getting. So, be completely honest with yourself. You may have become complacent or satisfied with how you have dealt with problems in the past. It may be time to try something different.

➤ **Action Step 1**

- Take a moment to think about a time when something you were worried about did not happen. What was it? Summarize that moment in a notebook.
- Do you remember how quickly your emotions changed from uneasiness to relief? The things you are worried about today will all fit into God's overall plan for your life. Take a moment to concentrate on this truth. Then think of *one* thing you can do within the next twenty-four hours that will demonstrate to God, and to others, that you believe this. What will it be specifically and how will you do it? Write it down.
- Now, do this one thing in simple faith in His Word—and observe what happens. At the end of the day write down what you observed.

KEY CONCEPT 2

What seems to be a problem for you, sometimes one of even tragic proportions, will lead to unanticipated gains. The key is to turn "unanticipated" gains into *anticipated* ones. As a Christian you have every reason to anticipate and expect God to increase your wisdom, abilities, character, and strength through the experiences of life. When you visualize what you will be doing or saying before you act, you are taking the initial step into becoming solution-focused rather than problem-focused.

➤ Action Step 2

- Exercise your imagination in a way that brings greater appreciation for your present moment and situation. Try a "back from the future" exercise for yourself. Close your eyes and imagine you are very near the end of your life. Take a few minutes to see this moment clearly in your mind. Now hear God say to you that He has given you the opportunity to go back and relive one day. Prepare to look about you and discover that *this* day, with all its ups and downs, is that day. It is given because within it God will reveal Himself to you—through every moment and experience. Now, open your eyes and *see*. Use your imagination to look at family, friends, and situations with this new perspective. Enjoy them. These moments go by all too quickly. What do you notice?
- Throughout the rest of this day seek to enter into this mindset as often as possible. There will be times when you discover that you have slipped back into your normal routine. Pressures and deadlines have pulled you down or distracted you. Possibly you've become angry due to some setback or frustration. That's okay. In fact, it's supposed to happen. It serves as a reminder to you to *reacquire* through your imagination the remainder of the day as a gift to relive. "Look again!" What do you see? At the end of your day, write down what you observed as you did this.

chapter two

Roller Coaster Expert

I've learned that the most creative ideas come from beginners —
not the experts.

H. JACKSON BROWN

He who has lost confidence can lose nothing more.

BOISTE

Life is a little like a roller coaster—ups and downs, twists and turns, slowly going up only to come down fast. Just when you think you are safe, the roller coaster makes an unexpected sharp turn to the right or to the left. Let down your guard for a moment and . . . whack, you bang your head against the back of the seat. More interesting still are the reactions of those who are on the ride. Some are nearly paralyzed with fright, holding on with white knuckles. Others have their eyes closed, afraid to peek out at the world hurtling by—possibly angry with themselves for having gotten on—or with others for having brought them. Some are acting as if they haven't a care in the world—pretending that the ride is not scaring or surprising them in the least. Still others are laughing and throwing their hands into the air, trusting the roller coaster to bring them safely back to the terminal.

So goes life: round and round, twists and turns, ups and downs, never ending. We may find ourselves at times shouting out, "Is there any way off of this thing?" The answer is yes and no. The ultimate reality of life is that none of us will get out of here alive! For the time being, though, we need to learn how to ride this thing successfully, and in doing so, to become roller coaster experts. To do this we must realize that the answer lies within us ... not the ride. We will discover that the ride has been given to us for a specific purpose.

EXPECTATIONS

Jesus said, "Remain in me, and I will remain in you. No branch can bear fruit by itself; it must remain in the vine. Neither can you bear fruit unless you remain in me" (John 15:4). What is this fruit? I believe the apostle Paul's explanation is the best one. He wrote, "The fruit of the Spirit is love, joy, peace, patience, kindness, goodness, faithfulness, gentleness and self-control" (Gal. 5:22-23). It seems to me that the fruit of the Spirit declare the emotions of God Himself—at least as much as we can understand of Him. These "emotions" flow from His thoughts. God is good. Indeed, "there is none good but one, that is, God" (Matt. 19:17 KJV).

So also, His thoughts are good. Consider God's words through the prophet Jeremiah. "For I know the *thoughts* that I think toward you, saith the LORD, *thoughts* of peace, and not of evil, to give you an expected end" (Jer. 29:11 KJV, italics added). It is because God is good, and His thoughts proceed from this goodness, that His fruit is so healthy ... His emotions so full. Thus, Jesus taught us, "I have come

> The fruit of the Spirit declares the emotions of God Himself—at least as much as we can understand of Him.

that [you] may have life, and have it to the full" (John 10:10). There is nothing halfway about God. What He gives, He gives fully.

Jesus makes it clear: to have this emotional fullness, this fruit, we must "remain" in Him. What does it mean, to remain or "abide" in Christ? The New Testament was originally written in Greek, and the word used here is *meno*. In this context it means to "stay" in a relationship with Jesus. Yet, it also includes a sense of "expectation." It is as if we were children again, waiting for our birthday or for Christmas to arrive. When we were little we could actually *feel* the anticipation. Do you remember? Our expectations for that special day, and the anticipation it brought, were closely related. The strength of our expectations heightened our sense of anticipation. We remain in Him with an expectation that something good is going to happen.

As we remain in Him, the greater truth is that He remains in us. He is transforming us through the renewing of our minds (Rom. 12:2). This renewing has to do with the actual repairing and restoration of our thought patterns. It represents a full renovation of our thoughts resulting in a transformation, a metamorphosis, a change from one form of life to another. We change from having a mind of confusion to having the mind of Christ. Like the caterpillar to the butterfly, so also is the dramatic change within the mind of a growing Christian. As Paul declared, "Therefore, if anyone is in Christ, he is a new creation; the old has gone, the new has come!" (2 Cor. 5:17).

ONLY ONE STREAM

The importance of this *renewing* cannot be overstated. It is only by becoming "roller coaster experts," managing the twists and turns of life with a clearly focused mind, that our salvation becomes evident. There are some who mistakenly believe that if we punch our ticket on Sunday mornings and try to be a nice person, we will automatically become a mature Christian. This approach to Christian faith is tragically false. Although becoming God's son or daughter happens as quickly as we receive Jesus as our Savior, becoming a mature Christian is something altogether different. It takes place as we develop spiritual habits and come into a daily, conscious agreement with the Holy Spirit's renovation project—our mind. This is what is meant by the phrase, "walking in the Spirit" (Gal. 5:25).

There are some who mistakenly believe that if we punch our ticket on Sunday mornings and try to be a nice person, that we will automatically become a mature Christian.

C. S. Lewis illustrated this idea in one of his wonderful children's stories from the Chronicles of Narnia. The stories take place in a land called Narnia that was created by Aslan. Aslan is a powerful Lion who, in this story, is a type of Jesus Christ. In one of the volumes, *The Silver Chair,* a young girl named Jill is transported out of World War II England into this land of Narnia, not knowing how.

After a time she becomes quite thirsty and is looking for water. In the distance she hears a stream....

> The wood was so still that it was not difficult to decide where the sound was coming from. It grew clearer every moment and, sooner than she expected, she came to an open glade and saw the stream, bright as glass, running across the turf a stone's throw away from her. But although the sight of the water made her feel ten times thirstier than before, she didn't rush forward to drink. She stood as still as if she had been turned to stone, with her mouth wide open. And she had a very good reason: Just on this side of the stream lay the Lion....
>
> "If you are thirsty, you may drink," a voice said....
>
> For a second she stared here and there, wondering who had spoken. Then the voice said again,
>
> "If you are thirsty, come and drink."...
>
> It was deeper, wilder, and stronger; a sort of heavy, golden voice....
>
> "Are you not thirsty?" said the Lion.
>
> "I'm dying of thirst," said Jill.
>
> "Then drink," said the Lion.
>
> "May I—could I—would you mind going away while I do?" said Jill.
>
> The Lion answered this only by a look and a very low growl....
>
> "Do you eat girls?" she asked fearfully.
>
> "I have swallowed up girls and boys, women and men, kings and emperors, cities and realms," said the Lion. It didn't say this as if it were boasting, nor as if it were sorry, nor as if it were angry. It just said it.
>
> "I daren't come and drink," said Jill.
>
> "Then you will die of thirst," said the Lion.
>
> "Oh dear!" said Jill, coming another step nearer. "I suppose I must go and look for another stream then."
>
> "There is no other stream," said the Lion.

This truth is as straightforward as this simple children's story: It is only through the renewing of our minds that we are transformed. There is no other way, there is no other "stream." We must become the experts on our lives, taking full responsibility for our thoughts, emotions, and behaviors. I am reminded of a story that former president Ronald Reagan once told. He had an aunt who was very kind to him and liked him a lot. One day she took him to a shoe cobbler and told the cobbler that she wanted him to make a pair of custom shoes for young Ronald. The cobbler asked, "Do you want square toes or round toes on the shoes?" Ronald hemmed and hawed; he didn't know what he wanted. The cobbler said, "That's all right, come back in a couple of days and tell me, and I'll make them for you."

A couple of days later the cobbler saw Ronald and said, "Do you want square toes or do you want round toes on your shoes?" And Ronald said, "I don't know." He said, "Well, come in a couple of days—your shoes will be ready." President Reagan said that when he picked up his shoes one shoe was square-toed and one was round-toed. The shoe cobbler looked at him and said, "This will teach you never to let people make your decisions for you from this time on." And Ronald Reagan said, "I learned right then, make your decision; if you don't, someone else will."

MENTAL HEALTH EXPERTS

You see, we now live in a society of experts. For example, I once received an advertisement encouraging me to subscribe to a certain mental health magazine. On the outside of the envelope were the words "Isn't your happiness worth just one dollar a month?" I must admit, I was interested. I figured mine might even be worth a buck and a half, so I opened the letter. There, written in bold script across the top of the first page, were the words "It's worth the small cost just to know you're really okay!" I see! If I subscribe to this mental health magazine I will be taking the first step toward my true happiness—and it will only cost me a buck a month! More than that, I will discover if I am "really okay." So for a nominal fee I can let the experts tell me if I am normal or not. Of course, hidden in this subtle marketing strategy is the assumption that the editors and writers of this magazine are completely reliable experts on what is and what is not normal.

As a counselor I have had numerous persons complain to me that they went to a therapist with a reasonably clear view of what they were having difficulty with. The therapist viewed himself as an expert on mental health, thus they were led to believe that their difficulties were actually symptoms of deeper dysfunctions. From this point on, the *expert* was in charge. If you are not comfortable with the expert's diagnosis, you may be labeled as being in denial. It all seems so professional: a treatment plan, diagnosis, medication, and prognosis.

This reminds me of some of the religious "experts" that Jesus had to contend with. On one occasion, "One of the *experts* in the law answered him, 'Teacher, when you say these things, you insult us also.' Jesus replied, 'And you *experts* in the law, woe to you, because you load people down with burdens they can hardly carry, and you yourselves will not lift one finger to help them'" (Luke 11:45–46, italics added). Labels from the world of mental health lock us into a self-fulfilling prophecy about our families and ourselves. We get so loaded down with disorders and dysfunctions that we can no longer trust the path as God unfolds it before us, much less *see* it.

You are not only called to be a roller coaster expert, but you are coming into conscious agreement with the true Expert on your life. God is at work in you, but you need to consciously look for evidence of His activity. Often by recalling the most obvious and foundational truths, we see evidence of His hand on our lives. For example, we don't often think about the air we breathe. Yet the Creator of both air and lungs makes His presence and work known every time we inhale and exhale.

So what clues are available for you to uncover the work of His Spirit? Professional therapists will often focus on all the wrong issues. They want to explore the problems. Instead, there are solutions just waiting to be created in agreement with the Holy Spirit. The apostle Paul wrote, "By the grace God has given me, I laid a foundation as an expert builder, and someone else is building on it. But each one should be careful how he builds. For no one can lay any foundation other than the one already laid, which is Jesus Christ" (1 Cor. 3:10–11).

A 350CC REKIKYCLE

We do not always understand why we do what we do—so we find ourselves looking to the experts. Perhaps it is just because the workings of our brain are so mysterious. I remember when my oldest son Nathan was about a year old. He astonished my wife and me one day by pointing to a motorcycle and declaring confidently, "Rekikycle!" It was one of his first words . . . sort of. It reminded me of my first experience with a motorcycle. I was about twelve. A pal of mine had recently purchased a 350cc Honda and confidently gave me permission to "try her out!" I had ridden a smaller motorbike once before, but I was not prepared for the power I was about to experience. Of course I failed to inform my buddy that I was far from an expert on a motorcycle. He asked me if I could ride, and like most boys I simply replied, "What? Are you kidding? Of course I can!" I didn't have a clue.

I got on the motorcycle, feeling the power of the engine beneath me. I revved it a few times just to show my friend that I knew what I was doing. Then I gunned it! The next thing I knew the front wheel was off the ground, and I was moving far too fast—falling backward. The motorcycle went right out from under me, I landed with a thud on my back, and the 350 flipped over and came to a stop about ten yards away. Needless to say, my disbelieving friend stood over me with his hands on his hips, looking at me with a level of disgust only twelve-year-old boys would understand. I never got a second chance on his motorcycle.

What happened? At age twelve I simply was not prepared for that much power. God has created our brains with an incredible amount of power, way too much for us to control on our own. Now, I believe God has a plan for helping us to naturally grow into such power, but we, His creation, have thrown out the instructions with the Instructor, in a sense saying to God, "What? Are you kidding? Of course I can handle that!" But we really do not have a clue.

We get thrown off the motorcycle again and again each day. And when that happens, we blame anything and anyone. We become frustrated because the power we want to control is controlling us. We wind up on our backs, gasping for breath in the dust every time. In reference to maintaining the self-control needed to govern our physical bodies, the apostle Paul wrote, "I beat my body and make it my slave so that after I have preached to others, I myself will not be disqualified for the prize" (1 Cor. 9:27). The brain, being the key to the physical body, needs to be brought into subjection to the will of the mind through the Spirit.

This failure to control our most powerful resource happens to every member of the human race every day. It is one reason why we should not overly depend on experts in mental health—especially those who are separated from God in their minds. How can they help others when they are lying on their backs in the dust? Even some Christian counselors fall into this "expert" mode if they are not careful. Instead, the primary purpose of Christian counselors should be to help persons get unstuck and on track with God. Thus the apostle John wrote, "I am writing these things to you about those who are trying to lead you astray. As for you, the anointing you received from him remains in you, *and you do not need anyone to teach you.* But as his anointing teaches you about all things and as that anointing is real, not counterfeit—just as it has taught you, remain in him" (1 John 2:26–27, italics added).

> The primary purpose of Christian counselors should be to help persons get unstuck and on track with God.

Then as now, it is the Holy Spirit whom we have received who will teach us how to go forward in our lives (John 16:13). He may choose to use human teachers or counselors to remind us of this (Eph. 4:11–14), but their purpose is to assist the only true Expert: God. Once we are moving forward, He will be a light to our path (Ps. 119:105).

THE MASTER OF THE RIDE

As roller coaster experts, we begin to learn that the answers to life's riddles are not found in knowing everything we can about the ride, nor in finding experts who can explain the ride to us. Rather, the answers are found within ourselves as we trust the Expert and as He instructs us through the ride. The ride of life becomes our education.

Keep in mind, the ride must have a *track*. This track, no matter how many ups and downs and twists and turns it may have, still has a purpose—a destination. As we move along this track of life we begin to observe and recognize our forward movement. We *are* making progress, but we have to consciously look for signs of it. We begin to learn that even the unexpected twists and turns of the track still lead us to our destination, our goal. The track will reveal the way we must go to get there. It is a guide, educating us in the step-by-step process necessary to proceed out from beneath the heaviness of our personal problems.

As the roller coaster proceeds firmly down the track, its movement characterizes our forward progress. Even when we have dry times, when we seem far away from

> **Even when we have dry times, when we seem far away from God, He, as the Expert on our lives, continues to guide us.**

God, He, as the Expert on our lives, continues to guide us. Now, this concept of the track is no different than the metaphor of the "path" found so often in Scripture. Consider these words: "Because of your great compassion you did not abandon them in the desert. By day the pillar of cloud did not cease to guide them on their *path,* nor the pillar of fire by night to shine on the way they were to take. You gave your good Spirit to instruct them. You did not withhold your manna from their mouths, and you gave them water for their thirst" (Neh. 9:19–20, italics added). Also, "You have made known to me the *path* of life; you will fill me with joy in your presence, with eternal pleasures at your right hand" (Ps. 16:11, italics added).

You will receive guidance from God in a variety of ways while you are on the track. The unexpected turns will no longer fill you with anxious feelings, nor will setbacks fill you with hopelessness and despair. Instead, the ride will become as a teacher to you, and you will become the student, a learner, being educated by the Master of the ride.

SOME KEYS TO THE RIDE

So how does this education happen? Of course, much is discovered only through twenty-twenty hindsight. That is, as Christians, when we walk in the Spirit, things just start to "work out on their own." Thousands upon thousands of Christians have found this to be true in their own lives. Knowing this offers a large measure of peace for those who live by faith, but it does not always help us with here-and-now decisions. Although life *is* an education, we still need to come deliberately into one accord with this training process. The key to mastering life is found in knowingly and purposefully coming into agreement with the Master.

> The key to mastering life is found in knowingly and purposefully coming into agreement with the Master.

One of the tools I use to do this is called a scaling question. Over the years, Christian counselors have used scales to determine a variety of things, all with one purpose in mind—to purposefully come into agreement with God and His unfolding of your life and your relationships. For this reason, I call them tracking scales. That is, they are scales that help us to visualize the track, or path, that God's Spirit is leading us along—and to keep track of our progress. They present us with some of the keys to the ride.

The Bible says, "Where there is no vision, the people perish" (Prov. 29:18 KJV). The primary feature of a tracking scale is that it enables us to visualize both an outcome and the steps along the way to it. Thus, they are used to visualize forward motion, to help us see the progress we are making, and to clarify the picture of change. In this sense they *organize* the vision for us. We are able to visualize both where we are and where we are going.

Tracking scales are used to measure numerous characteristics. They can encourage hopefulness, determine our willingness to work toward solutions, clarify our self-concept and self-esteem, and assess our commitment to relationships, to name just a few.

The value of a tracking scale is in how we use it. It helps us to create goals, and reveals our progress toward them. The basic form of a tracking scale is shown in the following question: "On a scale from one to ten, where ten means how you want things to be, and one means the worst that things have been, where would you say you are right now?" Keep in mind, the number you offer does not represent an absolute. It simply helps you to get a new view of your own situation. It is a starting point from which we can begin the process forward—no matter where we place ourselves on the scale. Let us look together at a number of areas where people often get stuck. Our goal in utilizing these tracks is to visualize how to get *unstuck,* and then to take the first step toward getting back on track.

Assess your own willingness to move forward regarding whatever problem you may be wrestling with.

How many times have you been stopped dead in your tracks by blaming others for your situation or condition? No matter how tempting this response to the problem may be, the result is always a loss of personal power. It is really rather simple—we need to focus first on what we can change. If you are not careful you will give up what you have control over, that is, your response, to try to change what you often have little or no control over, the situation. Your goal must be to focus on your *responses,* for it is here that God is primarily teaching you. In this way you will examine yourself first as the apostle Paul instructed (2 Cor. 13:5). Examine your own perceptions and weigh them against God's intention.

> **Your goal must be to focus on your response, for it is here that God is primarily teaching you.**

Begin by writing down or visualizing your problem or situation. Then ask yourself the following question: "On a scale from one to ten, with ten meaning I will do anything to solve my problem, and one meaning I will blame the situation or others for my problem, where would I put myself today?" Take a moment to think about this. Where you place yourself on this scale is entirely up to you. You have no reason to exaggerate or to be overly hard on yourself. Keep in mind, you are only showing *yourself* where you stand.

Now, what will *you* be doing differently when you move to the next number? For example, if you believe you are at a five, what will you be doing differently when you are at a six? It is important to think of this in as concrete a fashion as possible. You want to create a vision of your future where you are taking greater action to solve your own problem. The goal is to initiate a pattern for future success—rather than focusing on past failures. Remember, vague goals are hard to visualize and even harder to accomplish. Specific goals will provide for you a sense of how you will know when you get there.

What if I were videotaping you as you begin to act on your next number up the scale. What will I see you doing differently? There is a need for some caution here. You may be tempted to say what you would not be doing. "I would not be yelling so much" or "I would not be so angry." Okay, so what *will* you be doing instead? How *exactly* will you be doing this? Keep in mind, your primary concern will be how *you* will be doing this—not what others will be doing. God is working in their lives according to His own sovereign intention. The matter before us today is what He is doing in *your* life. In regards to family and friends, it will be helpful to take note of how they respond to you when you are deliberately doing a bit of the solution. By this I mean, what do you *observe* about them as they react to your changes? In general, what differences in your behavior do you *notice* when you are acting in a way that moves you a step up on the scale?

Keep in mind, the emphasis is on *doing* and *observing*. What actions or things will *you* be *doing* differently. How you feel is not being ignored or denied, but I have learned that *it takes less effort to act your way to a feeling, than to feel your way to an action.* God cannot steer a ship that is not moving. Once you are moving, coming into agreement with God's intention, your emotions will catch up. Your task is to now focus on your actions, specifically acting out a part of the solution that has been clarified.

Discover how to encourage and envision forward progress.

After you begin to observe some change, no matter how small, and you are growing in your willingness to take responsibility for your own progress, ask yourself the following question. "On a scale from one to ten, where ten represents how you hope your life will be when you solve your problem, and one means how bad things were when they were at their worst, where would you say things are today?" Once the decision is made to truly act on what you have envisioned you will discover an increased ability to see new possibilities—*actually seeing what your life will look like without the problem*. What did you do to be at the number you have chosen? Again, what will have to happen for you to move to the next higher number? How *exactly* will you be doing this? As before, your primary concern is how *you* will be acting.

> *Utilize tracking scales to monitor your starting point and progress in a variety of areas.*

- In your commitment to a relationship, begin by asking yourself, "On a scale from one to ten, where ten is 'I will do anything to improve this relationship,' and one is 'I have given up on this relationship,' where would I put myself at the moment?" What will have to happen to move to the next higher number?
- In your desire to clarify specific goals, begin by asking yourself, "On a scale from one to ten, with one meaning 'I don't feel like I can get any of this work done,' and ten meaning 'I feel like I've got it all together with my work,' where would I say I am today?"
- As you seek a better view of yourself and try to assess your self-esteem, begin by asking yourself, "On a scale from one to ten, with ten meaning the kind of person I always wanted to be, how close would I say I am to ten today? What is the closest I have ever come to ten?" Now, on a second scale of one to ten, with ten meaning "I'm very happy with my place on the first scale," and one meaning, "I really dislike where I am on the first scale," where would you be today? What will have to happen for you to move

up on the first scale? What will it take for you to make that happen just a little bit? What else?

- To encourage a greater communication of commitment in marriage, begin by asking yourself, "On a scale from one to ten, with ten meaning 'I am totally committed to my marriage,' where would you say you are today?" On the same scale, how much do you think your spouse wants this marriage to succeed? What will your spouse have to notice different about you in order to say that you are moving up to the next highest number? What do you notice about your spouse when you do so?

- To create a clearer vision of your future without the problem, take your one to ten response to any of the above scales and ask yourself, "Since I am a *four* [for example] on the scale of wanting to succeed, let me imagine that over the next two weeks I have moved to a *six* on the scale." What will be happening differently then? What will you have done to move yourself from a *four* to a *six*? What else will be different then? Describe more of that.

Once you have begun the process I have just described, following four straightforward, "commonsense" key steps will lead you to success:

- Do a small piece of your envisioned goal.
- Carefully look for what works.
- Deliberately do more of what works.
- Always observe what takes place when you do so.

In this fashion, God will begin to lead you into a more disciplined lifestyle, one in which you are taking greater responsibility for your own development. This acceptance of responsibility will put you into the very heart of the transforming intention of the Holy Spirit. You are becoming a roller coaster expert, mastering life with the Master of the ride.

Key Points and Action Steps for Personal Application

KEY CONCEPT 1

You are not called only to master life, you are called to come into conscious agreement with the Master of life. God is at work in you, but you need to consciously look for evidence of His activity. As you become more willing to look for clues to this work of God's Spirit, you will receive guidance from God. The unexpected turns of life will no longer fill you with anxious feelings, blaming others for setbacks, or filling you with hopelessness and despair. Instead, life will become as a teacher to you, and you will become the student, a learner, being educated by the Master.

➤ Action Step 1

- On the scale below, with ten meaning you will do anything to solve your problem, and one meaning you will blame the situation or others for your problem, where would you put yourself today? Take a moment to think about this. Where you place yourself on this scale is entirely up to you. You have no reason to exaggerate, or to be overly hard on yourself. Keep in mind, you are only showing *yourself* where you stand.

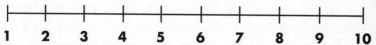

- What will you be doing differently when you move to the next number? Write your answers in your notebook. For example, if you believe you are at a five, what will you be doing differently when you are at a six? It is important to think of this in as concrete a fashion as possible. You want to create a vision of your future where you are taking greater action to solve your own problem.
- If I were videotaping you as you begin to act on your next number up the scale, what will I see you doing differently?

There is a need for some caution here. You may be tempted to say what you would not be doing. "I would not be yelling so much" or "I would not be so angry." Okay, so what *will* you be doing *instead?*

- How *exactly* will you be doing this? Keep in mind, your primary concern will be how *you* will be doing this—not what others will be doing.
- What do you *observe* about family and friends as they react to your changes? What do you *notice* that is different when you are acting in a way that moves you a step up on the scale?

KEY CONCEPT 2

Life has been given to you for a specific purpose. Your expectations will grow stronger as you hold within your heart God's intention for you. "For I know the plans I have for you, . . . plans to prosper you and not to harm you, plans to give you hope and a future" (Jer. 29:11). Jesus has come to give you life, and for you to have it "to the full" (John 10:10).

➤ Action Step 2

- It is only through the renewing of your mind that you can be truly transformed. There is no other *stream.* Today, begin to take a greater responsibility for your thoughts, emotions, and behaviors. As you do so your mind will be renewed, your physical brain actually becoming healthier. Deliberately look for new possibilities to emerge. Write down what will be the first sign to you that you are taking greater responsibility for your thoughts, emotions, and behaviors.
- What will your first step look like when you are doing this?
- What will your family and friends notice about you that is different when you take this step?
- Do a little of this on purpose and notice what happens. Write down what you noticed.

chapter three

A Stuck Disorder

God cannot give us a happiness and peace apart from Himself, because it is not there. There is no such thing.

C. S. LEWIS

Lately there has been a great deal of talk regarding how we define emotional disorders. Many of the daytime talk shows actively seek out those who are in distress in order to attract an audience. Although a disreputable practice, the American viewing public continues to tune in, so the producers of such shows will keep on bringing them to this hungry audience. Men and women of faith should never watch such human manipulation. Yet issues regarding mental health in one form or another affect us all. Perhaps Mom is "clinically depressed" or Dad is having "panic attacks." Grandma is "bipolar," and of course Aunt Helen has an "anxiety disorder." Certainly that teenager across the street must have a "personality disorder." You are "codependant" and Uncle Eddie has an "intermittent explosive disorder." Even Junior is "ADD" and "learning disabled." And everyone needs medication.

How have these labels come into such ready acceptance and popularity—even within the church? The manual that doctors and therapists use to guide their understanding of symptoms and help them in making a diagnosis is called the *Diagnostic and Statistical Manual of Mental Disorders,* now in its fourth revision (DSM-4). Within its pages hundreds of disorders are classified and organized according to their symptoms. Those mentioned above are just a few. Thus, we have a well-intentioned instrument that nevertheless views all emotional difficulties through what is wrong, damaged, missing, defective, incomplete, and inadequate—focusing only on these symptoms as criteria for describing mental health.

SYMPTOMS OR STUCK?

I am looking forward to the day when the DSM–25 comes out. It will be a much thinner manual, actually only one diagnosis to consider: STUCK! For the vast majority of people, symptoms actually point to a breakdown of options or possibilities. They have what I call a "Stuck Disorder."

> A "Stuck Disorder" is a mind-deadening inability to picture or work toward a way out.

Various fears, lack of family support, broken relationships, difficulties on the job, being out of work, and so forth, have all come together at a particular moment—resulting in a mind-deadening inability to picture or work toward a way out.

Whatever it is, it has resulted in a focus on problems, and given birth to various types of uncomfortable emotional feelings. How do we get stuck? To explain this I need to take a moment to illustrate how the brain works. Although much of the brain's functioning is still a mystery, more is being understood every day.

A BABY'S BRAIN

What does a baby see when he or she is born? Not much really. Everything is a blur. Mainly, the baby seeks to focus on eyes, connecting them to soothing sounds. Research indicates that at birth a baby's eyesight is 20/400, but rather quickly, within three to six months, connections between neurons in the visual cortex bring the baby's sight to 20/40 or better. Yet the baby's environment remains a blur. The reason everything remains blurred is that babies, as well as adults, see with their brains, not with their eyes. A baby's brain has not received enough sensory data to make much sense of what is being seen. For example, an infant looks at a couch, but sees only colors and shapes—even though the child's eyes are working quite well. In time, with more input from other senses such as touching, smelling, tasting, and hearing, this infant will *see* the couch. Until then he or she is "stuck" in this blurry vision of the world. The way to getting "unstuck" is to continue the natural development of the human brain from within a loving and supportive environment—all senses working to bring information into the cerebral cortex, each layer of data creating a context for the next.

This process is unending. We are always growing. The question becomes, are we aware of this process of growth? Keep in mind, this is a physical process, created by a loving God. The data brought in by your five senses goes into a physical location, connections and neural pathways forming constantly. Yet, at times, we do not keep up with the process of our own development. As was discovered through examining the children raised in Romania's orphanages, left alone without love and affection, this lack of human touch and interaction caused actual physical dysfunction within their brains. In many cases this led to physical dysfunction within their bodies as well.

This is the same process at work in us today. At certain times of our lives we are literally saturated with problems. The ability of our brain to keep up by creating the necessary neural pathways and connections is hindered; thus we become overwhelmed. We feel unable to cope. We are stuck, powerless to visualize options or solutions. The result is a physical change in the brain's chemistry—its neurotransmitters. We experience this as a change in our feelings—feelings of depression or anxiety for example. Basically, our senses have become unable to bring in enough of the right kind of data, the data that gives us new perspectives on our struggle. The "connections" have yet to be made. We are therefore overwhelmed, unable to "see the couch."

HOW DO YOU SEE?

In most cases, what is actually happening when we are experiencing "emotional disorders" is that we have not yet developed the mental ability to deal with this new set of problems. From a biological point of view you are at the limit of your neural pathways. Yet, this is also a spiritual problem because you were created to have enough access into God's thought patterns that you should not develop such difficulties. Thus, spirituality and the way God intended the mind to develop become one and the same thing. Certainly, who you are, and how you develop in this present life, is who you are going to be in the age to come. It could be that there will be stages of growth throughout eternity, but it begins here. Thus, life is an education for eternity—an education that begins in earnest with your new birth in Jesus Christ.

So, how we *see* this present life becomes essential. Again, Jesus often said, "For those who have eyes to *see* and ears to *hear*..."—such individuals will enter and live within the context of the Kingdom of God. Keep in mind, Jesus knew our eyes and ears are simply data receivers, not data processors. This is a metaphor for saying: all those who think God's thoughts will experience God's emotions, that is, the fruit of the Spirit (Gal. 5:22). Seeing becomes *"seeing"* when our minds can quickly make the connection from a present challenge or setback to a potential solution or outcome—which flows out of God's intention. Yet, this cannot happen until our brain actually has established the necessary "neural pathways."

THE LADY

Consider this picture. What do you see?

Boring, E.G., 1930.
"A New Ambiguous Figure,"
American Journal of Psychology,
42, 444.

Some will see an old "hag," while others see a young woman. What you see says little about your subconscious. Indeed, the concept of a "subconscious" is severely overrated. Rather, this drawing simply shows the limitations of your present neural connections. If you cannot see both the old hag and the young woman, look in the appendix—then return to this spot.

Now look at the picture again and you notice that you can easily see both the old hag and the young woman. Indeed, you can effort-lessly move from one to the other. Just as the baby could not "see" the couch, so also you could not "see" both women in the picture. Yet, now you can. Why? Your brain has learned how to "see" the whole picture. Even though your eyes were seeing the picture, they were not "seeing" it. Now they are. Good for you! You just changed the actual physical structure of your brain.

> The only approach that is beneficial is to be able to recognize that you are stuck, to know how to get unstuck, and to know how to get back on track!

Actually, you do this all the time—except when you are stuck! Then, like most of us, you either blame someone else for being stuck, or you blame yourself. Neither is helpful. The only approach that is beneficial is to be able to recognize that you are stuck, to know how to get unstuck, and to know how to get back on track! Most constructive solutions flow from this simple approach.

THE MIND OF CHRIST

What is the difference between the mind and the brain, and does it matter? Some say they are exactly the same; nothing else exists other than cells. Others have said the mind contains our ideas and images, while the brain holds the cells, electricity, and chemicals. Certainly the two interact with each other constantly. When we are praising and rejoicing with our mind, our body releases cells into the immune system that increase the health of the brain. Probably, the brain is more than the mind. Just because the brain is functioning does not mean that the mind is fully alert and effec-tive. Some have implied that the brain is like the computer, and the mind is the word processing program.

A friend of mine humorously suggested that the real issue is between the flesh and the spirit. He went on to say that since the word for flesh in the New Testament refers to meat, and the word for spirit refers to wind or air, that the true distinction is between being a "meat head" or an "air head"! If that were the case, when I was living more as a "meat head," I was simply living a functional life; my brain was working, but my mind was not truly alive and alert. Since I have been born of the Spirit of God my mind has been made alive in Christ through my new birth. But, this new mind has also affected my brain's cells, chemicals, and electricity, that is, the health of my brain—and the development of neural connections that now help me to *see* in a new way.

The Word of God states that we are a "new creation" in Christ (2 Cor. 5:17); we are not to be conformed to this present world but be transformed by the "renewing of our minds" (Rom. 12:2); we are to bring "every thought" captive to Christ (2 Cor. 10:5); and most important—we have the "mind of Christ" (1 Cor. 2:16). I believe these are not referring to religious dogma but rather a physical reality: our minds are being literally renewed.

Every human being has his or her own unique personality, each graciously planned by God's creative Spirit and uniquely formed by its genetic blueprint and environmental experiences. Yet, even though our personalities are formed, our minds (our reasoning capabilities) are just starting to develop. As it matures, the renewed mind in Christ will help its owner's personality to function according to God's will. In this fashion, true Christian character is being formed. But how does the renewed mind mature? Part of the answer is discovered in what we hold to be true—what we believe.

What we believe, we become. If we believe in a lie, we are formed by that lie. If we believe a truth, we are formed by that truth. If we choose to believe Satan's lies and live outside God's truth, we choose darkness and become empty inside, the mind responds dysfunctionally, and the character is corrupt. The prophet Hosea spoke of such a choice when he wrote, ". . . they [some within Israel] consecrated themselves to that shameful idol [Baal] and *became* as vile as the thing they loved" (Hos. 9:10, italics added). Conversely, when we choose to take God at His word and live in His light, our mind matures and our character becomes more like His own—now being revealed through our unique personality.

Tied into our beliefs are our expectations. If our expectations are on what only this present age can deliver, we receive only what this present age can give. If our expectations are on God, we can receive what only God can give. Thus, Jesus said, "Do not store up for yourselves treasures on earth, where moth and rust destroy, and where thieves break in and steal. But store up for yourselves treasures in heaven, where moth and rust do not destroy, and where thieves do not break in and steal. For where your treasure is, there your heart will be also" (Matt. 6:19–21).

Think of it this way. God's perfect design for how our brain is supposed to work has been given to us in Jesus Christ. He is our pattern, the re-creator of our minds. When God's Spirit helps us to truly *hear* and concentrate on what Jesus said—both personally and through His prophets and apostles, we are actually grafting His thoughts

Christ is being literally, physically, "formed in us."

into our own. Thus, Christ is being literally, physically, "formed in us" (Gal. 4:19). His thought patterns re-create our neural network, like an anti-virus program on a computer, making new pathways, and actually forming within this skull of ours the mind of Christ.

Let me add that the mind of Christ is not yet fully formed in us, although it is forming. The apostle Paul states that we *have* the mind of Christ. This is true in the same way that we even now are sanctified and glorified (Rom. 8:30). We are, *in* Christ—not in ourselves. For example, some years ago I was in Cuba, ministering in the refugee camps. I was a United States Navy Chaplain then, and during a sermon I took off my long-sleeved military jacket and gave it to a little boy who was about six years old. This immediately made him very famous with the other children, as he wore it proudly—his hands totally covered by the long sleeves. Then, through a translator, I explained that in time this little guy would grow *into* the uniform. Through the years he would grow physically and eventually fill a uniform that appeared ridiculously large on him at the present time. I did this to illustrate sanctification and the mind of Christ. We are already "wearing" them, for we are in Christ. Like the uniform on this child, sanctification is much larger than we can possibly imagine—for it is Christ Himself. And we are in Him. Eventually, as we grow, we grow into what we already have. We grow in grace, in sanctification, and in the mind of Christ.

As adults, our minds have developed to the point that we are exploring this universe in ever-increasing detail. Yet, we have just scratched the surface of what we shall be. As superior as our ability to see is to a little child, consider how much more our Lord's is than ours. The prophet Amos spoke of God wishing to reveal His thoughts to us (Amos 4:13). Our ability to see what God sees, to think God's thoughts, (at least as much as our human frames are capable of) results in our experiencing God's feelings—for feelings naturally flow from thoughts. Yet, to not see, to not think God's thoughts, is to get stuck in our own perceptions of any given situation.

Thus, Paul taught us that we reap what we sow. He explained that in our sowing to the flesh—our human nature apart from God, our own self-centered perceptions—we reap corruption. But in our sowing to the Spirit—God's nature in us, our acceptance of God's perceptions—we reap eternal life. This is why we cannot simply do as we please. What we sow, we actually do reap. The flesh does battle with the Spirit. As Paul wrote,

> Those who live according to the sinful nature have their minds set on what that nature desires; but those who live in accordance with the Spirit have their minds set on what the Spirit desires. The mind of sinful man is death, but the mind controlled by the Spirit is life and peace; the sinful mind is hostile to God. It does not submit to God's law, nor can it do so. Those controlled by the sinful nature cannot please God. You, however, are controlled not by the sinful nature but by the Spirit, if the Spirit of God lives in you. And if anyone does not have the Spirit of Christ, he does not belong to Christ. (Rom. 8:5–9)

Jesus is the way, the truth, and the life. Eternal life must be more than length of life. Rather it is the *kind of life Jesus lived*—and demonstrated on earth. I do not believe Jesus was ever depressed or anxious. That is not to say He was never sad or angry. He was certainly both. He wept over Jerusalem and the rich young ruler, both having turned away from Him. He was angry at the money changers in the temple and the so-called religious leaders of His day. Yet, His emotions were in keeping with His Father's thoughts. Fear and hopelessness were noticeably absent. What are your emotions in keeping with? If you truly desire the mind of Christ, you must turn yourself over to the tutelage of the Holy Spirit, to be actively aware of your training each day, and to apply this training in a deliberate fashion. All solutions proceed from being in agreement with Him. So, what is stopping you from doing this today?

Key Points and Action Steps for Personal Application

KEY CONCEPT 1

A "Stuck Disorder" is a mind-deadening inability to picture or work toward a way out of a present difficult situation. The way to getting "unstuck" is to purposefully continue the natural development of the human brain, all five senses working to bring information into the cerebral cortex, each layer of data creating a context for the next. Your brain will then establish the necessary neural pathways so your mind can learn to swiftly make a connection from a present challenge or setback to a potential solution or outcome—one that is more in agreement with God's intention.

➤ Action Step 1

- Whenever you are not thinking God's thoughts you will get stuck in your own perception of any given situation. God's intention is to develop your character to be like Christ's. In this way, your character will bring out the best of your unique personality. To do this, it is essential to recognize—daily—what is forming your character. The communications and entertainment industry such as television, radio, novels, movies, video games, sports, and so forth, all market to your brain a world of ideas—some healthy, others unhealthy, many useless. This input actually goes someplace. It takes up a physical location in your brain, making trillions of neural connections, thereby forming much of your inner conversation. Keep in mind, you are becoming what you say to yourself each day. (Remember, if your expectations are on what only this present age can deliver, you can receive only what this present age can give. If your expectations are focused on God, you can receive what only God can give.)

- On the scale below, where ten means how much you are influenced by God's thoughts and communications, and one means how much you are influenced by the communications and entertainment industry, where would you say you are right now? (Honestly consider how you spend the hours of each day.)

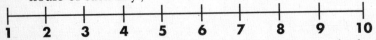

- What will you do to move yourself to the next highest number on the scale?
- What will be different then?
- Do a small piece of what you have envisioned and carefully look for what works. Deliberately do more of what works, and observe what takes place when you do so. As descriptively as you can, write down what you notice.

KEY CONCEPT 2

God's intention is for each of His children to have the mind of Christ (1 Cor. 2:16), not simply as a spiritual concept but as a physical reality. As your mind matures, through both your walk with Christ and the "doing" of His Word, God's perfect design for how your brain is supposed to work will unfold. Jesus, as the pattern, is the re-creator of your mind. He is being "formed in you" (Gal. 4:19)—His thought patterns shaping your neural network, making new pathways, and actually forming within your cerebral cortex the mind of Christ.

➤ Action Step 2

- The apostle Paul taught the church how to maintain a greater awareness of God throughout each day. Pause for a moment and read about the "armor of God" in Ephesians 6:10–17. This armor is a metaphor for Christ Himself, and when it is deliberately "put on," God's Spirit will help form the "mind of Christ" within you. Carefully consider the following points, and then utilize the scaling question:

1. The "primary" pieces of armor (vv. 14–15), truth, righteousness, and peace, must be deliberately "put on" every morning and often throughout the day—*always* in the order given! When you do so, you will sense an inner peace that comes from thinking God's thoughts of truth, and reviewing His gift of righteousness to you. The "belt" of truth represents what you believe (and know to be true) about God. We worship in "spirit and truth" and the truth about God is that "God is love." The "breastplate" of righteousness is what God believes (and knows to be true) about you. He loves you without conditions and intentionally plans for your success. Today, and every day, you can trust Him. With these twin truths in place, your emotional peace, that is, an absence of fear and anxiety, is established. You are mentally and emotionally prepared to see the world through God's eyes. These three pieces must be put on consciously and actively each day. Visually put on each piece, and mentally think through its implications.

2. Only after the primary armor is in place are you able to utilize God's "battle armor" (vv. 16–18). The three pieces of battle armor are faith (to resist the daily "whispers" from the Enemy—the Father of Lies—that attack your peace); salvation (the hope, expectation, and assurance of God's intention being fully realized in your life); and the applied Word of God (brief memorized verses that open

your mind to God's influence—His truth, righteousness, and peace in the midst of each day's activities and struggles). Again, put each piece on consciously, actively, and visually—mentally thinking through its implications for you.

- On the scale below, where ten means you are putting on the armor of God each morning and often throughout each day, and one means you are not putting on the armor of God at all, where would you say you are right now?

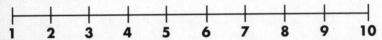

- What will you be doing differently at the next highest number on the scale? Be specific.
- What will be different then? Again, specifics.
- Do a small piece of what you have envisioned and carefully look for what works. Deliberately do more of what works as you move up the scale, keeping track of your progress. Note what takes place when you do so, and write out your observations. Develop the habit of putting on the armor of God each morning before leaving home, and consciously keep it on throughout the day.

chapter four

Change Is Inevitable

It is not possible to place your foot in the same stream twice.

HERACLITUS

The only person who likes change is a wet baby.

MARK TWAIN

One of the most common errors in a Christian's life is the belief that our ability to grow spiritually is somehow linked to the intensity of our environmental pressures. When life grows more difficult, it becomes harder to concentrate on our faith. Thus, we may begin to wait for life to "get better" before we live out the implications of what we believe. We are waiting for something to change, not realizing that change is *inevitable*. Heraclitus is credited with the saying, "It is not possible to place your foot in the same stream twice." As the water is always in motion, so also change in our lives is constantly occurring. As we come more into agreement with God's Spirit, it becomes helpful to think *how* the change will occur, rather than *when* it will occur.

As we come more into agreement with God's Spirit, it becomes helpful to think *how* the change will occur, rather than *when* it will occur.

So what stops us? Again, we get stuck. God cannot steer a ship that is not moving, when we begin to move He will help us to harness the winds of change. To master life we must follow in the direction of the Master. Yet, we do have an enemy. He is the Father of Lies and the archdeceiver. His hatred of God is all consuming. Unable to hurt God he seeks to hurt God's children—hoping to break the heart of God. Starting with Jesus, his goal has been to deceive, demoralize, and destroy. As he failed with Jesus, so also he will fail with you. But his traps are set.

Deception is like that—a trap. Imagine walking through a forest. Suddenly you see a half-covered rope noose on the ground. It is attached to a branch that is bent down low to the earth. You realize that if you step into the noose, the trap will be sprung. The noose will swiftly close around your leg, and before you realize the gravity of your error, you will be hanging upside down from the tree. Of course, being intelligent, you laugh at this lame attempt to trap you. The noose is clearly visible, and there is no way you are going to step into it. So you **Deception seen is not deception at all.** decide to step around the noose. But, as soon as your foot touches the ground . . . swoosh! There you are, hanging upside down from the tree. The purpose for the first half-hidden noose was to cause you to step into the second completely hidden noose. You see, *deception seen is not deception at all.*

THE ENEMY'S WHISPER

You may feel that you are mature enough to see through Satan's deceptions. Think again. Consider a little girl, perhaps seven years of age, playing in the park close to her home. She sees a kind-looking man who is searching for his little dog. He has the leash in his hand and is calling out for his lost puppy. She asks him what kind of dog it is, and he shows her a picture of a fluffy little white poodle with a pink bow in its hair. Slowly he leads her further and further away from the park as she helps this nice man look for his doggie. This child would never have gone with a stranger, but she will help a kind man look for his lost little dog. She is now another statistic, never heard from again. Why? Because this man knew how to deceive her; he found something that would disarm her parents' instructions. He was older and craftier. So also is the enemy of our souls. Satan is older and craftier than you or I, and, as such, is very dangerous. We *can* be deceived. If we think we cannot, we are in the greatest danger!

One of the primary tactics of the Enemy is to convince us that we cannot change. "Too set in your ways," he whispers into your ear. Perhaps you have heard this soft insinuation yourself. "Your husband will never change," or "Your son's heart will never return to you," or "You will always feel just as hopeless as you do today," or "You will never be good enough, or pretty enough, or happy enough, or thin enough," and so on. I recall an old Tom and Jerry cartoon in which Jerry the mouse wants to pull Tom the cat's tail. He is trying to decide what to do when a little devil mouse appears on his right shoulder. Dressed in red tights and with a pitchfork, he is egging Jerry on to pull the tail.

Then, over the left shoulder an angel mouse appears. "Do not do it," the little angel mouse is imploring. Keep in mind, there is no talking in these cartoons. The entire message is portrayed with pictures. Jerry finally decides to pull Tom's tail, probably because that is what this cartoon is all about. Yet, the battle for our will is not so different from that cartoon. Often we make our decisions based on which voice we listen to. The voice we listen to more often is the one that forms us. Although an audible voice is rarely heard, we still "hear" the hiss of the serpent in his lies and deceptions. But they are craftily presented. If not for God's still, small voice gently encouraging and strengthening us, we would easily be led into fear and hopelessness. But we choose which voice we listen to. In so doing, we learn the ways of faith and trust, and we learn how to harness the winds of change.

FRANCIS THE CAT

When I was five years old my family moved to Houston, Texas. We stayed there for three years, and when we left we brought with us many wonderful memories—and a little stray cat we named Francis. While in Houston I learned that Texans like to do everything big. I did not realize that this applied to cats as well. Well, this little kitten grew into one of the largest, nastiest alley cats you've ever seen—you know, the kind that Doberman pinschers run in terror from. As a child I knew not to move an inch if Francis had fallen asleep on my leg. My life was on the line. The patches of fur missing from his face were a testament to numerous pitched battles. When I was little Francis seemed like a giant to me.

Today I have discovered that I love kittens, but dislike cats. Maybe this is due to growing up with Francis. When he was first brought to our home, my dad, like so many other dads before him, said, "No way!" He did not want a cat, we were not keeping the cat, and that was his final word! Discovering the dilemma, my brothers and mom came up with a plan. We named the cat after my dad. How in the world can he throw out a cat that has his name? And even though my dad goes by Frank, somehow "Frank the cat" just did not sound right. Amazingly, the plan worked. What a pushover! Francis was now part of the family and when we moved to New York, Francis came along.

As Francis got older he became less frightening. Now, war-torn and slowing down quite a bit, his many battles were catching up to him. But what he had lost in strength and meanness, he had made up for in patience and wisdom. I remember one time, just to see what his reaction would be, my childishness got the better of me. You know what happens when you pet a cat—they begin to purr. Well, I was petting Francis, and he was purring contentedly. But, just as he was drifting off into a deep rest I reversed my strokes—moving firmly against the fur! Now you would expect a cat to get pretty upset by this, perhaps arching its back, hissing, and maybe even scratching. Yet, old Francis just got up, slowly turned around, and laid back down facing the opposite direction! I guess he figured that since the petting had reversed course, he would turn his body around to get back into a good purring position.

Now I do not know how this aged, battle-scarred cat figured it out, but his wisdom is sometimes lost on us mere humans. When everything is going well, and life is "petting us" so to speak, our purring is loud and contented. Then, out of nowhere the petting reverses course. What was going well either evaporates or actually begins to create other difficulties and challenges. Instead of following Francis's lead, we do the opposite. Claws come out, hissing starts, and our emotions are filled with anger and blame. Yet, if we were attentive to this old cat's lesson we would get up, turn around, and lie back down—allowing the problems to begin to teach us the lessons of God. Thus James writes, "Dear brothers and sisters, whenever trouble comes your way, let it be an opportunity for joy. For when your faith is tested, your endurance has a chance to grow. So let it grow, for when your endurance is fully developed, you will be strong in character and ready for anything" (James 1:2–4 NLB).

I think this is what the prophet Habakkuk was referring to as well when he wrote, "Though the fig tree does not bud and there are no grapes on the vines, though the olive crop fails and the fields produce no food, though there are no sheep in the pen and no cattle in the stalls, yet I will rejoice in the LORD, I will be joyful in God my Savior. The Sovereign LORD is my strength; he makes my feet like the feet of a deer, he enables me to go on the heights" (Hab. 3:17–19). Though his prayers did not seem to be answered in the way he had anticipated, he would continue to rejoice in the Lord. In so doing God made

> You can view change as a continuous reality, a part of life's purpose, not to be feared but placed in subjection for the Master's use.

his feet like the feet of a deer; that is, his confidence in God's intention became even more surefooted. When you "turn around" as Francis did, and rejoice as Habakkuk did, your problems actually form and develop you. You will begin to see, as it is happening, the education of life. Now you are walking in the Spirit in agreement with God's intention. You can view change as a continuous reality, a part of life's purpose, not to be feared but placed in subjection for the Master's use.

BIOLOGICAL MEMORY

But what about those unwelcome thoughts that often intrude into our daily activities? Just when we think we are on track and enjoying victory in God's plan, our emotions shift, and we feel anxious or depressed. Where are these emotions coming from and what can we do about them?

Often the feeling is the result of a memory from our recent or remote past that has been triggered without our knowing it. For computer buffs this would be a little like having an old program open all by itself while we are working on a project in a different program. We would glare at the screen, scratch our heads, and wonder what gives. But what if we had the technology to link our computer programs up to the human brain? Then when a program or file opens it would not only bring us the information on the screen, but we would *feel* the information. If this was possible, then imagine the confusion when, right in the middle of a project, an old file opens all by itself. We would experience an unbidden change in our emotional state—one that now interferes with our present responsibilities and activities!

I think you would agree that this would take some getting used to, yet our brain does this every moment of the day without any effort whatsoever. It is receiving millions upon millions of bits of data through our five senses and utilizing them for the numerous "programs" we have running. Yet, all of these thoughts are based on neural pathways that function

> "When your faith is tested, your endurance has a chance to grow" (James 1:3 NLB).

through neural transmitters, or hormones. These are our emotions, each transporting specific bits of data. So we can be operating our present "programs," that is, our daily activities, and one of our senses will bring in some data that triggers an old file. This file immediately opens, and is transported by its neural transmitter—its emotion. The process is not difficult to understand, it is just that we are usually not aware that this is what is happening. The result is that we accept the negative "triggered" emotional state as a true emotion, and begin to act upon it.

In a sense the brain is acting like a time machine, the triggered thought bringing a memory from hours, days, months, or even years before. At the speed of light that memory is back in your thoughts—and the emotion with it. Yet, that emotion does not belong in this present moment. It passed through time in less than a blink of an eye to be opened once again in the present.

Although I believe God has a clear reason for such an incredible ability, when not understood, such power brings with it a potential for great emotional distress. Yet what is its purpose?

What reason could there be for such ability? One example of God's purpose can be discovered and demonstrated in the apostle Peter's life.

A JOURNEY THROUGH TIME

At Peter's darkest moment he denied Jesus. His fear overtook him and, like a knife, it cut deeply into his hopes and dreams. Listen to how John's gospel describes it: "The guards and the household servants were standing around a charcoal fire they had made because it was cold. And Peter stood there with them, warming himself. . . . Meanwhile, as Simon Peter was standing by the fire, they asked him again, 'Aren't you one of his disciples?' 'I am not,' he said. But one of the household servants of the high priest, a relative of the man whose ear Peter had cut off, asked, 'Didn't I see you out there in the olive grove with Jesus?' Again Peter denied it. And immediately a rooster crowed" (John 18:18, 25–27 NLB). In the horror of that night Peter had denied his Lord three times.

Then after the resurrection Jesus came to Peter, who had chosen to go fishing with some of the other disciples. He instructs them to lower their net over the side of their boat, and the result is a miraculous catch of fish. Then Peter, in his enthusiasm, jumps out of the boat and swims to shore to reach Jesus—a deeply emotional response. *A memory had been triggered within his thoughts, one that was linked to this emotion of excitement and adventure.* What was the memory? Of course it was this catch of fish. It recalled the first time he met Jesus, and his commission to fish for the hearts and souls of humanity (Mark 1:16–17). How was the memory triggered? It was triggered through numerous sensory data. Some would include the smells and sights of the great catch of fish. Can you imagine as he watched the sun reflecting off the sea as the water was churning and sparkling with the great mass of fish? Smelling and tasting the sea against his face, Peter's emotions must have been shaken with the memory of his calling to follow Jesus—not to be out fishing.

Yet his "journey through time" was not yet complete. John continued his gospel by writing, "When they got there, they saw that a charcoal fire was burning and fish were frying over it, and there was bread" (John 21:9 NLT). When Peter reached the shore Jesus had a charcoal fire burning. It was alongside this same kind of fire, with its unique smell, that the resurrected Savior said three times to Peter, "Simon son of John, do you love me?" (John 21:15–17 NLT). Notice that Jesus does not call him Peter, but rather Simon—his name of flesh rather than the new name given him as part of his call. Three times he questions Peter's love and commitment—one for each denial.

Yet the memory of Peter's denial was already assaulting his thoughts, for he stood once again next to a fire of coals. There was the sight of the fire burning, the smell of the charcoal, his blood racing and heart pounding—*the same sights, smells, and feelings from the night of his betrayal.* Jesus had brought him back to the moment of his fear and confusion, utilizing all of the sensory information that Peter's brain would have stored up of that terrible night. And there the loving hand of God calls for a renewed confession of faith and love, thus bringing forgiveness and healing, as the wall of discouragement and oppression falls from around the heart of Simon Peter.

CHEMICAL WARFARE

Thus, God has a purpose for placing within the human brain the capacity to retrieve memories and past emotions. Because humanity fell away from God, we now need to relearn this purpose, bringing it into subjection to God's Spirit. Yet, we must keep in mind that the *Enemy* seeks to manipulate this ability, as he does with all God's good gifts. Through the deliberate manifestation of malevolent evil, the natural body can be at war with itself.

So in a sense, when we are wrestling with "intense or heavy" emotions we are entangled in an internal form of "chemical" warfare. Our neurotransmitters are being affected negatively. Yet even in the middle of this inward struggle with our emotions, we must remember that God's kingdom is more than our momentary, internal chemical battle. Remember, in Christ we have died and risen, our eternal life having already begun in God's eyes. As the apostle Paul wrote, "Fight the good fight of the faith. Take hold of the eternal life to which you were called when you made your good confession" (1 Tim. 6:12).

We fear that the intense or "heavy" emotions will never leave, but again, change is inevitable. As quickly as they come, they can go away. It is the fear of such emotions that maintains and feeds them.

When we feel discouraged, anxious, angry, or hurt, we fail to recognize the behavior or thought that these emotions transported, or even what triggered such a thought. Having entered into an "older" neural pathway, one where the hurt or anxiety was originally born, we connect this emotion to our present experience of life. By doing so, we fail to perceive and appreciate the numerous exceptions to these negative emotions. Like a cartoon, we flip the separate pictures of our lives so quickly that it seems like a seamless whole.

Yet, each day brings new thoughts and emotions—and we can begin this day, this moment, with the thoughts and emotions of Christ. Often, we do not recognize the many moments when life is truly satisfying: watching rain fall or the sun rise; hearing the sounds of birds floating on the wind or the symphony of children's laughter; feeling a cool breeze against your face or the warm embrace of a friend; tasting cold, refreshing water on a scorching summer's day or hot cider on a crisp winter's night; smelling fresh bread baking or the pleasing aroma of a kitchen on Thanksgiving day. Giving thanks and practicing God's presence are essential to enjoying life. They also help us recognize, as it is happening, the change that is everywhere, always around us.

> We fear that the intense or "heavy" emotions will never leave, but change is inevitable. It is the fear of such emotions that maintains and feeds them.

THE GOD OF CREATION

So how can we stay "connected" to the truth of God's presence? Sometimes the heavy or painful emotions remind me of a groove in an old mattress. We may start our sleep near the edge, but morning will find us stuck in the groove once again. Like the mattress we may sleep on every night, continuously harmful thoughts will lead to emotional states of depression or anxiety, which in turn lead to harmful behaviors. This pattern, when continually repeated, becomes readily triggered by sensory data we gather in the course of our daily experiences. So what can we do?

One approach is to not try so hard to force such thoughts away from our minds. This simply intensifies their hold on us. It is like trying to get an annoying tune out of your head. The more you try, the more it persists in its hold. Yet, when your mind becomes engaged with other interests, the tune usually falls away through lack of use. I remember when I used to teach classes by using transparencies on an overhead projector. I would put four or five together, joined together at the top. The first would give a part of the information I wanted to present, but would leave blanks and even partial inaccuracies. But as I added transparencies, the meaning would change. Blanks were filled in, and seemingly obscure designs became clear. Each new transparency would alter the teaching just a little—until the final meaning became evident. So also, we can alter the picture our past transparencies are projecting into our minds. We do this by deliberately adding to it—thus changing its story. One transparency can be laid over another to reveal a new meaning. Thus the old meaning falls away on its own through lack of use. The new has superseded the old.

Although God's ultimate revelation of Himself is through His Son, He also reveals much about Himself through the universe He has made.

To do this you must first recognize the inevitability of change—and God's intention for the change to be one that increases hope and personal competence. Then, look for clues of His activity in your life, both past and present. As you do you will be aided by what God has so obviously given to you, that is, your five senses. Although God's ultimate revelation of Himself is through His Son, He also reveals much about Himself through the universe He has made. Through creation His voice can continually be heard and His presence felt. Unfortunately, all too often we tend to look for God in the mysterious and miraculous.

This was the tempter's strategy when he tried to deceive Jesus during their battle in the wilderness (Luke 4). Why not perform the miracle of turning a rock into bread, or of jumping off the pinnacle of the temple in Jerusalem and mysteriously being upheld by angels? Jesus rightly rejected such temptations, yet we are tempted in the same way today. We desire the mystery of religious faith—perhaps something *we* understand that others do not.

Actually, God is more often found in the obvious and the ordinary. When we begin to understand this idea, we discover that nothing is quite so ordinary and obvious as it first appeared. We will come to recognize God's presence more often through the means He has made available to us, again, our five senses. Consider these words from Scripture:

- "*Taste* and see that the LORD is good; blessed is the man who takes refuge in him" (Ps. 34:8).
- "How sweet are your words to my *taste,* sweeter than honey to my mouth!" (Ps. 119:103).
- "*Hear* now, O Israel, the decrees and laws I am about to teach you. Follow them so that you may live and may go in and take possession of the land that the LORD, the God of your fathers, is giving you" (Deut. 4:1).
- "*Look* at my hands and my feet. It is I myself! *Touch* me and see; a ghost does not have flesh and bones, as you see I have" (Luke 24:39, Jesus after His resurrection).
- "And the people all tried to *touch* [Jesus], because power was coming from him and healing them all" (Luke 6:19).
- "To [those who are perishing apart from God] we are the *smell* of death; to the other, the *fragrance* of life" (2 Cor. 2:16).
- "For I tell you that many prophets and kings wanted to *see* what you see but did not see it, and to *hear* what you hear but did not hear it" (Luke 10:24).

The Word of God is overflowing with references to our five senses. Why then do we use our senses so rarely in a deliberate fashion to recognize the hand of God in our lives? Again, we have fallen into the deception of seeking God in the mysterious and the miraculous. Yet, God is everywhere present. As King David declares, "The heavens declare the glory of God; the skies proclaim the work of his hands. Day after day they pour forth speech; night after night they display knowledge. There is no speech or language where their voice is not heard. Their voice goes out into all the earth, their words to the ends of the world" (Ps. 19:1–4). The fruit of such a view of creation is found in how David completes this psalm of praise. He writes, "May the words of my mouth and the meditation of my heart be pleasing in your sight, O LORD, my Rock and my Redeemer" (Ps. 19:14). By *seeing* God everywhere present, David's meditations, that is, his daily thoughts, become pleasing to God.

As I was writing these words I became hungry. Not wishing to stop, I took a banana and prepared to eat it quickly. Yet, as I took my first bite I had to pause. I must have been quite hungry because the taste of this marvelous fruit washed through me . . . and I began to offer thanks. As I finished with a drink of cool water I paused again to thank God that He had created me with the ability to appreciate this refreshing quality of the drink. Another sensation of God's goodness took hold of me. I did not offer thanks out of duty, a

God is more often found in the obvious and the ordinary.

quick routine prayer over my meal, but rather as an honest reaction to how wonderfully God has made me . . . and His banana and water. I would never have thought of building the human race in such a fashion, yet God has. In this and millions of other ways, He has planned for our joy and fulfillment. Yet, I would have missed it had I not paused to "taste" the fruit.

After all, why did God put the taste in it in the first place? There are certainly more "practical" ways to take in the necessary sustenance. Why? Because God said taste was good. That is, it would taste good, and it was a good idea to create taste (Gen. 1:11–12)! As I continue to recognize this, I enter into a closer walk with my Father. If I failed to do so, I would be like a foolish child who doubts his next meal even though his parents have always provided for all his needs. In his doubts he feels distant from his mother and father, finally blaming them for his feeling of alienation. Many of us do this to God as well. But God will speak to you in ways you can easily understand. He is not trying to confuse you and stay mysterious. The opposite is true. He communicates His love and guidance constantly through His Son, His Spirit, His Word, and through all of His creation.

The apostle Paul powerfully declared this truth when he wrote, "For since the creation of the world God's invisible qualities—his eternal power and divine nature—have been clearly seen, being understood from what has been made" (Rom. 1:20). Thus, Paul teaches the necessity of praise and thankfulness within the everyday issues of life. As Paul continues, consider the progression away from God when we fail to praise: "For although they knew God, they neither glorified him as God nor gave thanks to him, but their thinking

> As we glorify God as God, giving thanks to Him in the "obvious and ordinary," we receive a sound mind, our thinking becomes purposeful.

became futile and their foolish hearts were darkened. Although they claimed to be wise, they became fools and exchanged the glory of the immortal God for images made to look like mortal man and birds and animals and reptiles" (vv. 21–23). So then, as we glorify God as God, giving thanks to Him in the "obvious and ordinary," we receive a sound mind, our thinking becomes purposeful, our hearts are filled with God's light, and wisdom becomes our companion.

When the prophet Elijah was depressed God spoke to him, saying, "'Go out and stand on the mountain in the presence of the LORD, for the LORD is about to pass by.' Then a great and powerful wind tore the mountains apart and shattered the rocks before the LORD, but the LORD was not in the wind. After the wind there was an earthquake, but the LORD was not in the earthquake. After the earthquake came a fire, but the LORD was not in the fire. And after the fire came a gentle whisper. . . . Then a voice said to him, 'What are you doing here, Elijah?'" (1 Kings 19:11–13). God is often the God of the gentle whisper—the "still, small voice." As we recognize God's presence "through what has been made," we begin to become more aware of His "gentle whisper."

COMING TO OUR SENSES

Let me encourage you to make more deliberate use of your senses in a way that recognizes God in all things: His love in the cool of a breeze, His voice in the sound of a sleeping child's breathing. You need to connect yourself to the present moment. What do you see? What do you hear? What do you feel? What do you smell? What do you taste? Give thanks and rejoice that you see in color rather than simply in black and white, that you taste the peanut butter *and* the jelly, that you hear the sounds of children playing and not only your own voice complaining, that you can smell the rose and the freshness of a newly fallen snow and do not have a perpetually stuffed nose, that you can touch the face of someone you love and feel their touch in return. Ask anyone who has lost one of these blessings and you will learn how much you have to be thankful for.

Give thanks and rejoice that you see in color rather than simply in black and white, that you taste the peanut butter *and* the jelly.

All too often our problems cloud out the obvious touch of God in the everyday miracle of life. What we label anxiety is actually our present fears thrown to the future. That is, the near or distant future is believed to contain nothing more than an extension of the present or past experience of discomfort—resulting in the physical sensation of anxiety. So also, depression offers up a vision of future hopelessness and helplessness. Or, perhaps the past contains pain and disappointment. In either case, past or future, we are not living in the present with Christ. Our thoughts are continually pulling us away from our "walk" with God's Spirit in the present. Keep in mind, *life is the miracle!* It is constantly changing, revealing more and more of the Savior for those who train their senses to look for His presence.

When you put down this book, pause and listen. Ask yourself what you hear. How many different sounds can you identify? Name each one. What do you feel? Do you feel the clothing on your body? Why didn't you a moment ago? Do you feel your back against the chair or sofa? Your own heart beating? What do you see? Name each and give thanks. Do you recognize that you are walking and living *in* God's Spirit?

In Matthew 6:26 Jesus taught us to look at the birds of the air. The word Jesus used means literally to take a good look, to discern clearly, and to carefully observe. This is true of all our senses. The next time you sit outside, listen, look, taste, smell, and feel the world around you. On the way to work, while washing the dishes, as you mow the lawn, in your coming and your going—taste and see that the Lord is good. To help me remember to do this, I call these actions "present moment connectors" (PMCs). They help us to add new "transparencies"—effectively changing the meaning of that which has been. Love is rewriting the physical structure of your brain.

Let me add at this point that God's beautiful creation has been terribly marred by the fall of humankind. There is a malicious aspect to the world today. As a result of humanity's rebellion, its turn from the love of God, nature has been "subjected to frustration" (Rom. 8:20). Yet, in its tragic harshness the hope and love of God shines through—restoration is everywhere present. Perhaps your heart has been broken. God foresaw your loss, not planning it, but planning *for* it. All that is, all that ever shall be, has been created to give you the pleasure of experiencing God. Even your loss shall be healed in new and vibrant memories of

> **Love is rewriting the physical structure of your brain.**

God's presence—and an assurance that God does all things well. He has pledged to walk with you through any pain, with the intention of building and maturing you as His child. God will come to you in the soft breeze as well as through His Word. The breeze will confirm His Word even as He created a world that offers both a sunrise and a sunset. We are part of this world and this world is part of us. Walk as a part of it, not apart from it. Through your transformation into a true son or daughter of God even creation will someday be fully restored. The lion will lie down with the lamb.

The apostle Paul wrote,

> I consider that our present sufferings are not worth comparing with the glory that will be revealed in us. The creation waits in eager expectation for the sons of God to be revealed. For the creation was subjected to frustration, not by its own choice, but by the will of the one who subjected it, in hope that the creation itself will be liberated from its bondage to decay and brought into the glorious freedom of the children of God. We know that the whole creation has been groaning as in the pains of childbirth right up to the present time. Not only so, but we ourselves, who have the firstfruits of the Spirit, groan inwardly as we wait eagerly for our adoption as sons, the redemption of our bodies. For in this hope we were saved. (Rom. 8:18–24)

All of creation will teach you of God, even as it reveals His lessons each day. He is the Master of life, and His intention is for you to master life. He who loves you will not rest till whom He loves is perfected. Nothing is wasted. All has purpose. As He spoke to the prophet Isaiah, "Although the Lord gives you the bread of adversity and the water of affliction [that is, our instruction will be difficult at times], your teachers will be hidden no more; with your own eyes you will see them. Whether you turn to the right or to the left, your ears will hear a voice behind you, saying, 'This is the way; walk in it'" (Isa. 30:20–21). As you come into agreement with God's "teachers" throughout each day, acknowledging His presence, His wisdom, His humility, and being thankful, you will be led into a conscious recognition of the process of change in you. Even your most painful memories will be rewritten by Love. As you do so, your family, friends, associates, and even the strangers you may meet will recognize that you have been with Christ. Not all will respond to this favorably, but many will.

God instructed Moses to say to the people of Israel, "These commandments that I give you today are to be upon your hearts. Impress them on your children. *Talk about them when you sit at home and when you walk along the road, when you lie down and when you get up*" (Deut. 6:6–7, italics added). The reason children are to be instructed in this way by their parents is that this is how God instructs His children. This is true for us all. We are taught directly by the Spirit of God as we sit in our homes, walk along the road, in our lying down, and in our getting up. His lessons are continuous—if we will but see and hear what the Spirit is saying. So also will be our security and protection. God said to Moses, "See, I am sending an angel ahead of you to guard you *along the way* and to bring you to the place I have prepared" (Ex. 23:20, italics added). Never forget, it is "along the way" that God is teaching and guarding you.

You may wish to ask yourself about this. How will your family, friends, and associates know you have been with Christ each day? What will they observe about you, and how will you be able to tell they noticed? Also, what will be the first sign that you are changing in the way God wishes—to be more in agreement with His intention? As you begin to see this change in your mind's eye, begin to act on what you see. Remember, small change leads to larger change. Then watch carefully what happens next.

Key Points and Action Steps for Personal Application

KEY POINT 1

Change is constant. It is more helpful to think "how" the change will occur, rather than "when" it will occur. Change occurs, and it does so most rapidly in the midst of difficulties. The things you are presently calling "problems" are actually meant to form and develop you. They are bringing you the lessons of God. To receive this instruction you have to pay attention.

➤ **Action Step 1**

- During "problem" times you are always making choices. Unfortunately, you are often unaware of doing so. You are choosing which voice to listen to—God's voice or the voice of your own fears, which is oftentimes strategically enhanced by Satan. Successfully navigating change comes down to which voice you habitually listen to. The one you listen to more often will do the most to form you. Even though an audible voice is rarely heard, you can always discover which voice you have listened to by your subsequent thoughts, behaviors, and emotions. This week consider your thoughts, behaviors, and emotions. Are they negative, destructive, or discouraging? If so, which voice have you been listening to? Write down your observations.

- How will you recognize God's voice when He is speaking?
- What will you be doing differently when you challenge voices that are negative, destructive, or discouraging? (Remember, Satan will flee when you offer *firm* resistance, because he is a coward as well as a liar.) You can resist his lies by consciously submitting yourself to God and asking daily for His help. As the apostle James wrote, "Submit yourselves, then, to God. Resist the devil, and he will flee from you. Come near to God and he will come near to you" (James 4:7–8).

KEY POINT 2

The human brain acts like a time machine. Emotions can be experienced that were part of memories from hours, days, months, or even years before. At the speed of light that memory can be back in your thoughts, bringing the emotion with it. Keep in mind that this emotion does not belong in your immediate situation. It passed through time in less than a blink of an eye to be opened once again in the present moment.

➤ Action Step 2

- God's Spirit will bring healing to you through restorative thoughts. One way He does this is by triggering memories that lead you to repentance and healthy change. Keep in mind that the Enemy seeks to manipulate this ability, as he does all God's good gifts. Today, deliberately be more responsible in judging and critiquing your own present emotional state. Do not place too much trust in your momentary shift of emotions, but rather recognize them for what they are, and ask God to reveal to you His purpose in allowing memories to surface. If the memory does not lead you back to wholeness, as well as strengthening your Christian commitments, then you have every right to reject it as a manipulation by the Enemy to create fear within you. God perfectly loves you, and "perfect love drives out fear" (1 John 4:18). At the end of your day, write down your observations.

KEY POINT 3

Through a more deliberate use of our senses, we can learn to recognize God in all things. You need to connect yourself to the present moment. Give thanks and rejoice. Otherwise your problems will crowd out the touch of God in the everyday miracle of life, your thoughts pulling you away from your walk with God's Spirit in the present moment.

➤ Action Step 3

- Utilize your senses as "Present Moment Connectors" (PMCs). Take a slow, deep breath and pause. Ask yourself what you *hear*. How many different sounds can you identify? Name each one. What do you *feel*? Do you feel the clothing on your body? Do you feel your back against the chair or sofa, or your own heart beating? What do you *see*? Name each and give thanks. The next time you sit outside, listen, look, taste, smell, and feel the world around you. On the way to work, while washing the dishes, as you mow the lawn, in your coming and your going—taste and see that the Lord is good. Note what takes place when you do so. Write out your observations as descriptively as you can.

chapter five

Problems Complex?
Solutions Need Not Be!

A single event can awaken within us a stranger totally unknown to us. To live is to be slowly born.

ANTOINE DE SAINT-EXUPERY

I absolutely hate rattling noises in my car. Perhaps you know someone like me. We hear every little creak and groan. I can be driving in the car with my wife and family, perfectly content and at peace with the world, when all of a sudden I will hear it—the rattle. I immediately look to my wife and ask the same senseless question—"Do you hear that noise, honey?" Somehow, my wife never hears it. Yet, the rattle has now completely disrupted my trip and is, like an ancient water torture, slowly driving me insane.

Now, I am not speaking of engine noises. I leave those to a qualified mechanic. I am talking about rattles, clangs, squeaks, pops, and bangs! The kind that I hear and my wife either does not hear, or pretends not to just to push me over the edge. I can never find them because they only happen while I am driving, and I cannot ever seem to locate the source of the sound.

Sad to say, throughout my life I have only located one rattle. Some years ago I was convinced that something must have fallen into the console of our newly purchased, but used, minivan. After taking apart the entire console, I found a spoon. A spoon in my console! I knew something was there, and finally, I proved it. Of course, I never did get that console back on right. I guess I can always use the spare screws and bolts for something else. . . .

Isn't this how most of us are? We have a desire to get to the root of our problems—to find out what is causing that rattle. Somehow, if we can just find the rattle, we can fix this thing. But, what my wife knows, and what I am still learning, is that when I concentrate on that rattle, *it is all I can hear.* In fact, it becomes the focus of my conversation in the car and the center of my attention throughout the trip. I jokingly refer to these as the "rattles of the ride." They can affect my emotional well-being, as well as the way I treat my wife and children, and most of the time they represent something that I cannot change—at least not at that moment.

I have discovered in my counseling practice that a person's "rattle" does not always need to be found.

I have discovered in my counseling practice that a person's "rattle" does not always need to be found. I am not minimizing anyone's frustration or past trauma. The past needs to be discussed—just not focused on. In many cases, the problem cannot be fully defined, because different things mean different things to different people. Or as one friend said, "Various people perceive various problems in various ways." That is what makes some problems so complex. Meaning is perception. That is, what we believe we have seen becomes the truth for us.

When we consider that present-day difficulties often connect with trauma or disappointments from our past, or with fears regarding our future, it is no wonder problems can become so complicated. Then when we try to communicate our feelings and thoughts to others around us, who have their own perceptions—formed by their own past experiences and future fears—it should not be surprising that interactions become so strained.

It is the solution that needs to be clearly defined.

Rather than the problem, it is the *solution* that needs to be clearly defined. Instead of focusing on the rattles of the ride, let us ask instead what is different during the times when the "rattle" is *not* occurring. What are we doing differently when the problem is not happening? What do others notice about us during those times? In this way we begin the process of looking for the evidence that the Spirit has already placed in an individual's life: *clues to ways of getting unstuck.*

LABEL, LABEL, WHO'S GOT THE LABEL?

Another difficulty with focusing on the rattle is that we begin to find what we are looking for. This is true in our dealings with ourselves, as well as our dealings with others. I am reminded of a story I read regarding an experiment that revealed some of the dangers associated with using labels to describe people. Dr. D. L. Rosenhan, then professor of psychology and law at Stanford University, took a group of emotionally healthy people and admitted them to various psychiatric hospitals. The psychiatrists who met with them were simply told that each patient was "hearing voices." Once admitted, the new patients presented a thoroughly honest account regarding their mental state. He or she was truthful about everything except the experiment. Even though all of these pseudopatients would have been considered normal by society's standards, each was diagnosed as schizophrenic. One was also diagnosed as bipolar (manic-depressive).

> We usually find what we are looking for.

Keep in mind that each pseudo-patient in this experiment acted normally. Yet, once perceived as a person who was "hearing voices," their normal behavior was labeled as a charade—masking mental illness. Each was held from between seven to fifty-two days. Dr. Rosenhan did finally tell the hospitals of his experiment. He also informed them that he would attempt it again in the near future. What was the result of that information at the hospitals? Of the next 193 admissions, the staff found forty-one impostors. Interestingly, Rosenhan had not repeated the experiment. It is simply human nature to find what you are looking for.[1]

I am not implying that these psychiatric centers were deliberately negligent. Only that even the most objective and professional of us will usually see what we are looking for. That is why

---

[1] J. Striano, *How to Find a Good Psychotherapist* [Santa Barbara: Professional Press, 1987].

it is essential to also be looking for strengths—in ourselves and in others—and to learn from our encounters with God's grace. Also, by focusing on strengths, we are more in agreement with God's intention. Let me illustrate this important point with four stories from my counseling practice.

THE LITTLE GIRL WITH THE BIG MEMORY

Carolyn was a distressed parent who came to me for help with Heather, her eight-year-old daughter and only child. Mom was divorced for five years and was now in a relationship with a man who was very loving and kind to her daughter. Heather was very forgetful and inattentive. She would forget her homework quite frequently and would often ignore her mom when she spoke. This in turn had led to arguments, and arguments had led to punishments. Carolyn saw in her daughter some of the same difficulties she experienced in childhood and did not want Heather to fall into the same habits.

Mom asked her daughter's school counselor to test Heather for attention deficit disorder (ADD), which she had recently read about. This diagnosis seeks to describe two types of individuals. The first type is hyperactive. The second is inattentive. It was this second type that Carolyn saw in her daughter. Questionnaires were given to Heather's teachers and also to Carolyn. When she came to me, we scored these questionnaires and looked over them together.

I found it interesting that neither of Heather's teachers recognized a problem. It was their opinion that she was attentive enough—averaging Bs and Cs. Yet, Mom's answers regarding her daughter scored well above average, implying that Heather did indeed have a possible difficulty with inattentiveness. Since these tests were inconclusive, and before ordering other tests for ADD, I decided to give both Carolyn and Heather a simple task.

Privately, I spoke to Heather about her mom's belief that she was always forgetting things. Heather disagreed with her mom on this but admitted that she did *sometimes* forget things. Since she partially disagreed with her mom's view of her, I asked if she would like to prove her mother wrong. She liked that idea, and we made a simple plan for her to remember to bring her homework home every day after school so Mom would realize she could do this. She agreed to our secret plan. Then, privately, without telling Carolyn what Heather and I had agreed to, I asked Carolyn to deliberately look for *anything* Heather remembered this week, and to praise her for remembering it. She was not to focus on the things Heather forgot, only what she remembered.

The next time we met I asked Heather privately how her week had been. She immediately began to giggle. She explained that the school had given the Iowa Tests, so she had no homework all week! So much for my plans. Yet, it was the first thing she "remembered" to say to me—and with some satisfaction. Then I met with Mom. Carolyn was beside herself with curiosity. She had to know what I had done. Heather had been remembering *everything* all week. I never did let her in on what we had agreed to, preferring to be thought a genius. We continued this process for a few more weeks with other concerns, each time with similar results.

> I believe God's intention for you is good and that He has been preparing you for spiritual and emotional health.

So what happened? Among other things, Mom began to find what she was looking for! In so doing, she also reinforced it with approval, thus encouraging Heather to repeat such praised behaviors.

I believe God's intention for you is good and that He has been preparing you for spiritual and emotional health. You should be looking for evidence of this health. You will usually find in yourself, your spouse, and others just what you are looking for. This is the inherent problem with most mental deficiency labels. When we look for deficiencies—in ourselves or in others—we will usually find them, since we *all* have deficiencies to one degree or another. I prefer to not only look for strengths but also to assume they will be there as part of the sovereign work of God.

MARRIAGE COUNSELING OVER THE PHONE

A woman who was contemplating divorce called me for an appointment. Unfortunately, I was unable to see her that day, so we spoke for awhile, and I listened to some of her concerns. Since what we could accomplish over the phone was limited, we scheduled an appointment for the following week. Before ending our conversation I gave her a small assignment to prepare for our meeting. I asked her to observe—between now and when we were to meet—all the things in her marriage that were working, what she wanted to see continue. She was to develop a list of what she noticed and bring it with her when she came to see me.

A few days later she called and canceled the appointment, saying that she had taken my suggestion to heart. To her surprise she noticed a number of things in her marriage and about her husband that she wanted to see continue. She had also asked her husband to add his thoughts to the list. This resulted in a very positive focus on their respective strengths. They concluded that they wanted to give their marriage another chance. She thanked me for "being so helpful," and I let her know that I was available if she needed any assistance in the future.

> Whatever the problem may be that is worrying you, this problem does not happen all the time.

My advice to this wife and to you today is to remember that whatever the problem may be that is worrying you, this problem does not happen all the time. There are other good times. There are aspects of your life that you are happy with. The wife who canceled her appointment with me said that she had remembered things that brought back hope. She was going to wait awhile and see what would happen next. I encouraged her to focus on these things that gave her hope—the things that were working—and to do more of them deliberately. I also advised her to take note of what happens when she did so and to stay on track with this more positive approach to her marriage, that is, finding out what is working and doing more of it on purpose.

THE PROBLEM CHILD

A family that came for help a few years ago was experiencing difficulties with one of the sons. Mom and Dad came in, along with Jimmy (age ten) and Jonathan (age fourteen). Jimmy had been pointed out by his parents and brother as the source of most of the family's problems. They wanted to discuss *his* problems at length. No doubt many of these problems were right on target. But, during the course of the counseling session I watched Jimmy become more withdrawn from the conversation, and his eyes become more downcast, as the accusations piled up.

I decided to ask the family to consider the times when these problems did *not* happen. It did not take long before they had listed a number of areas where Jimmy was doing reasonably well. Even Jonathan entered in with a few things he liked about his little brother. What a transformation took place in Jimmy as the family's conversation shifted into this more helpful approach. I watched him sit up and enter back into the discussion.

I then asked what was different about those good times. What was different about Mom and Dad? How were they reacting to Jimmy when he was doing well? What were they doing differently? Also, what was big brother doing differently when he was happy with his little brother? Then I wondered what will Jimmy be doing when the family *really was* solving this problem? It turned out that it was quite similar to the things that he was doing that the family identified as working.

Without a doubt, this family's problems were complex. Also, everyone seemed to agree that the bulk of the problem was centered on this unhappy ten-year-old. In discussing Jimmy, we probably just scratched the surface. Yet, the solution was not found in the problem. The solution was to refocus on the times Jimmy was doing reasonably well, and to bring the family's attention to those times. Remember, whatever we focus on, we reinforce. The solution was already within Jimmy. Even the other family members recognized it and could say what it was when encouraged to do so. The real issue was to bring more of this solution-behavior out of Jimmy—to encourage it and reinforce it. This would have remained a nearly impossible task when the focus was squarely on *him* as the problem.

Are you listening more to the "rattles of the ride" than to God's Spirit?

The labeling and problem talk had been ineffective. The switch to a focus on "solution-conversation" began to move the family toward an awareness of times when the problem was not dominating the family. These in turn suggested possibilities for creating solutions. What was exciting is that these strengths flowed out of the life experience that God had already placed within this family.

THE DISRESPECTFUL STEPDAUGHTER

A very dramatic instance of change occurred recently with a thirty-eight-year-old husband who was trying to figure out how to be a proper father to his twelve-year-old stepdaughter. It seemed that they were always getting into arguments—and more often than not this baffled stepdad was unable to figure out how he got into them. He was sure of one thing. His wife's daughter was terribly disrespectful.

Now, you might imagine the complexities of a situation such as this. The young lady's emotional state could certainly be explored. So also the mom's expectations—which were strongly influenced by her life experience up to this point. Also, how was this aspiring dad raised? Was he shown enough affection by his father? As if this alphabet soup of unanswered questions were not enough, the arguments were now causing significant marital stress, as Mom was being pulled between the two antagonists. No answer was in sight.

Now all of these issues are both significant and complex. Certainly there are times when such meaningful issues should be explored, either in counseling or, better yet, in freewheeling family discussions. Yet, I noticed the passion of this stepdad's insistence on the issue of disrespect. He had no difficulty describing how his dad *compelled* respect from him when he was a boy— sometimes physically! At the end of our session I asked him if his dad's concept of respect had been helpful for him in growing up. He was quick to respond. He often hated his dad for it and frequently felt very distant from his dad. "But I sure did learn respect," he added, shaking his head.

I must admit I was curious to know more about this man's relationship with his dad. But that would have been a long winding road to go down, and it may or may not have led us back to the issue at hand. Instead, I made one simple suggestion before he left that day. I recommended that every time his stepdaughter showed what he considered to be disrespect, that he view it as immaturity. It was a simple suggestion, but his head slowly came up and his eyes focused on me. He began to laugh a little as something seemed to click.

As it turned out, this simple modification made a great deal of difference for him. He had been stuck in only one perception of his stepdaughter—one way of seeing. Yet, since her disrespectful comments or behaviors were actually manifestations of immaturity, this

Although a problem is complex, the solution does not have to be.

dad was now free to react to them as such. His changed reaction resulted in a new, somewhat softer, "counterreaction" from his stepdaughter. This in turn made possible a gentler "counterreaction" from her stepdad—and so on, and so on. Mom, sensing the change, also adapted to this new, calmer environment.

Although the problem *was* complex, the solution did not have to be. Also, this was only one solution. Others were still to be created. I also encouraged Stepdad to focus more on what was working now that he had changed this perception of his stepdaughter's disrespect, and to do more of that type of behavior *deliberately*. This kept the ball rolling, opening up even further opportunities for change. Now this family is on track to the future they imagined for themselves. With the "neural connection" made, new possibilities opened up. They were back into a greater agreement with God's intention, and His thoughts were working their way into their thoughts.

What is working in your life and in the lives of those around you? Are you listening to, and focusing more on, the "rattles of the ride" than God's Spirit? Quite often we do not realize the significance of our resources. As you begin to shift your perspective in this way, you may wish to ask yourself some other questions as well: *How are these good or better things happening? How can I continue to have these good things happen and to build on them? What strengths do I have that helped these "better" times to happen?* Remember, problems can be quite complex—but solutions need not be.

Key Points and Action Steps for Personal Application

KEY POINT 1

Often problems cannot be fully defined because different things mean different things to different people. Rather than the problem, the solution needs to be clearly defined. Instead of focusing on the problems, ask what is different during the times when the problem is not occurring.

➤ Action Step 1

- Remember that whatever problem may be worrying you, this problem does not happen all the time. There are other good times. There are parts of your life that you are happy with. Take a moment to consider how these good or better things are happening.
- What are you doing differently when the problem is not happening?
- How can you continue to have these good things happen and to build on them?
- Write down what strengths you have that helped these "better" times to happen.

KEY POINT 2

Each of us tends to find what we are looking for. Therefore, it is vital to look for strengths in yourself and in others. God's intention for you is good, and He has been preparing you for spiritual and emotional health. Look for evidence of this health. You will usually find in yourself, your spouse, and in others just what you are looking for.

> ➤ **Action Step 2**

- This week, observe all the things in your life that are working—what you want to see continue. Develop a list of what you notice. Try to do more of what is working.

chapter six

Touched by God

Heaven will solve our problems, but not, I think, by showing us subtle reconciliations between all our apparently contradictory notions. The notions will all be knocked from under our feet. We shall see that there never was any problem.

C. S. LEWIS

God is, and continues to be, thoroughly involved in your life. He has been, is, and will be active in the heart, mind, and spirit of all who will ever come to love Him or to know Him. God has truly and meaningfully touched you. At issue is whether you are going to trust what God has already been doing. When you assume God's presence in your life, you can begin to look for clues of His activity. You should presume they are there. What are some of the signs, or clues, of the activity of your heavenly Father in your life?

THE WRITING OF THE SPIRIT

The clue most often overlooked is what I call the "writing of the Spirit." The writing of the Spirit refers to times when God has entered the story of our lives, but we have not appreciated this significance. I believe such involvement is the norm, not the exception.

The apostle Paul wrote to the church at Thessalonica that God is already at work in our lives: "For this reason we also thank God without ceasing, because when you received the Word of God which you heard from us, you welcomed it not as the word of men, but as it is in truth, the Word of God, *which also effectively works in you* who believe" (1 Thess. 2:13 NKJV, italics added). Paul *assumed* that God's Word was already active in the lives of those he was writing to.

We are each a letter, being written by the Holy Spirit. As Paul wrote to the Corinthians, ". . . you are a letter from Christ . . . written not with ink but with the Spirit of the living God, not on tablets of stone but on tablets of human hearts" (2 Cor. 3:3). It is essential that we each specifically look for the writing of God's Spirit in our lives, rather than focusing on present or past problems. What are we not seeing that we should be seeing?

The Scripture continually reveals such an awareness of God. It depicts His entrance into human history, recording this writing in numerous lives. God's Word is given to teach us to be tenacious regarding the things of God, and to develop a mature hope in His intention for our lives. "For whatever things were written before were written for our learning, that we through the patience and comfort of the Scriptures might have hope" (Rom. 15:4 NKJV). So also, everything that was *written* in our past, by the Spirit, was written to teach us.

God is already at work in our lives.

In his book *The Great Divorce,* C. S. Lewis speculates that heaven works backwards (1946). That is, as we draw closer to the Spirit's intention for our lives, we begin to see His handwriting clearly revealed on our lives from birth—God reclaims the years the "locust has eaten" (Joel 2:25). The harvest represented the hopes and dreams of the land's owners. When the swarms of locusts devoured the harvest, they destroyed the longings and expectations of the families who lived there. So also, for many of us. Our dreams have been shattered—often while we were still children. We still seek to make sense of what has transpired. God will restore you by taking the beauty of His heaven and working it backward, reclaiming all your longings and wishes. You are being *rewritten* by God's grace. But, to recognize this writing of the Spirit you must exercise the creative imagination God has given to you. This is a gift from God and represents an aspect of our being made in His image.

HOW DO WE GROW AS BELIEVERS?

Much of traditional psychological teaching is influenced by theories of how we as human beings develop. These theories present stages of growth from birth through old age. Each stage of life has its tasks to complete. Thus, we have "stages" of education as children are growing. There are obvious similarities between children at each of these stages so comparisons can be made as to the progress of a child's development. Thus, when we say that a child is going through a "stage," everyone clasps their hands together and petitions God for the child's swift progression to the next stage!

One application of this teaching is in counseling. Many counselors believe that uncompleted tasks may emotionally lock us into a certain stage. Though we grow physically beyond that stage, we are immobilized emotionally due to this unfinished business. Clearly, we all have stages to grow through on our journey toward maturity, but I do suggest some caution here. This belief, though sound, may at times hinder or limit forward progress. Here is how that can happen.

Consider the infant raised by parents who were either abusive or never demonstrated love to the child. Children are very resilient. They learn how to cope. Often, they have no choice. Now, growing into adolescence, having learned to survive in an environment without clearly communicated expressions of love, this young person may doubt even genuine expressions of love and affection. These doubts negatively influence other adolescent decisions. In this way a destructive cycle begins—actions and counterreactions. These continue to create more cycles of negative actions and reactions—or *interactions*. Now the young person's actions, his growing doubts and emotional withdrawal, reinforce his parents' lack of affection or abuse, as well as alienating potential friends. The continuing abuse reinforces his emotional withdrawal—and so on and so on, one feeding off the other.

According to one theory, this child's future will be strongly influenced, if not determined, by these early experiences. So the child, now grown, will have great difficulty giving or receiving affection. He will need to go back and work through these earlier stages more successfully—gaining insight as to why he now withdraws from those who seek to get close to him. Although insight is usually helpful, this approach also may result in overfocusing on the past lack of affection, and its resulting interactions that are obstructing progress.

I wonder, is it possible that God is not limited to events that took place in our past, no matter how traumatic they were? If we believe the Bible, we believe God is eternal. Through His Word we understand Him to be omnipresent—all places at once; omniscient—containing all knowledge past, present, and future; and omnipotent — all-powerful. Together, these three describe and explain His sovereignty. Therefore,

> God is beyond our linear view of existence, that is, viewing life as a progression from beginning to end, one stage after another.

He is beyond our linear view of existence, that is, viewing life as a progression from beginning to end, one stage after another.

Let us assume for a moment each of us has stages to go through, each with its tasks. We can number these stages one through ten. Let us also assume that you are at stage five. Because of your relationship with a Sovereign Creator, is it possible to move forward from where you are, while incorporating the lessons from one through five in the process? Keep in mind that these lessons will reveal the writing of the Spirit, and will be based on His sovereign plan and loving intention for your life.

WHAT IS GOD'S DECLARED INTENTION FOR YOU?

Any biblical view of God's intention is established on your understanding of the devastating quality of sin, your former separation from God, your redemption, and now your new life in Christ. That is, it is founded on God's grace and sovereign plan for your life. God is at work in each human life. He has specific plans for you to grow and to prosper. Again, He spoke through the prophet Jeremiah saying, "'For I know the plans I have for you,' declares the LORD, 'plans to prosper you and not to harm you, plans to give you hope and a future'" (Jer. 29:11).

Thus, His deliberate intention is for difficulties and evil—past, present, and future—to accomplish good. In this same way, we learn from Joseph, whose brothers tried to kill him, and then sold him into slavery. He said, "But as for you, you meant evil against me; but God meant it for good" (Gen. 50:20 NKJV).

This is primarily true for those who live according to His intended *purpose*. As the apostle Paul wrote to the church at Rome, ". . . we know that in *all* things God works for the *good* of those who *love* him, who have been called according to his *purpose*" (Rom. 8:28 NKJV, italics added). By the way, it is essential for us to keep in mind that those who harden their hearts still live within God's intention, for from the same clay the potter can form some vessels for noble purposes and some for common use (Rom. 9:21). God will use the evil person just as He uses the Devil—to fulfill His ultimate intention. But, if the evil person returns to God, he will once again be an instrument for His noble intentions (2 Tim. 2:21).

As you become more fully aware and in agreement with His intention you will begin to recognize His writing in your life. God, speaking through the prophet Isaiah, said, "For my thoughts are not your thoughts, neither are your ways my ways. As the heavens are higher than the earth, so are my ways higher than your ways and my thoughts than your thoughts" (Isa. 55:8–9). That is, God's plan flows from a design infinitely greater than anything we now perceive. Therefore, our pre-

God's intention for us is what must form us.

sent perceptions of life must be critiqued in view of God's intention.

WHAT ARE GRACE EVENTS?

Along with God's writing in our lives, another clue to God's activity is what I call "grace events." These are our past problems, successfully encountered, that we should be utilizing in preparing us for the next problem. They reveal God's grace in the concrete issues of our lives, representing turning points. Unfortunately, we often fail to recognize the significance of what we have experienced, and therefore neglect what we have learned. C. S. Lewis once wrote that "... experience is such an honest thing. You may take any number of wrong turnings; but keep your eyes open and you will not be allowed to go very far before the warning signs appear. You may have deceived yourself, but experience is not trying to deceive you. The universe rings true wherever you fairly test it" (1955).

DAVID

Consider the story of David, that is, the David from the Bible. His is a story enjoyed by believer and nonbeliever alike. It represents courage and determination over brute force and violence, a victory of faith over seemingly insurmountable obstacles. What prepared David, as a teenager, to take on this kind of a challenge—the challenge of a Goliath? Let us enter in to the story at the point that David is speaking to King Saul.

> Then David said to Saul, "Let no man's heart fail because of him; your servant will go and fight with this Philistine." And Saul said to David, "You are not able to go against this Philistine to fight with him; for you are but a youth, and he a man of war from his youth." But David said to Saul, "Your servant used to keep his father's sheep, and when a lion or a bear came and took a lamb out of the flock, I went out after it and struck it, and delivered the lamb from its mouth; and when it arose against me, I caught it by its beard, and struck and killed it. Your servant has killed both lion and bear; and this uncircumcised Philistine will be like one of them, seeing he has defied the armies of the living God." Moreover David said, "The LORD, who delivered me from the paw of the lion and from the paw of the bear, He will deliver me from the hand of this Philistine." And Saul said to David, "Go, and the LORD be with you!" (1 Sam. 17:32–37 NKJV)

The fight between David and Goliath is where most of us think the story really gets interesting. Yet, for our purposes, the most fascinating information has already been given. Let us consider this for a moment.

When young David encountered the lion he had at least two options: He could hide or he could fight. The lion represents a *grace event*. A grace event is a planned crisis, prepared by the hand of a Master Teacher. It is only afterward that most of us become aware that we have passed through a turning point—and we have changed. I refer to these points as events of grace because they represent the primary intention of God's grace through the Holy Spirit for the Christian—to work upon our lives until "Christ is formed" in us (Gal. 4:19).

Viewed from this side of eternity these grace events look a lot like problems and tragedies. Yet, from heaven's perspective, they are grace events. If we could replay this encounter, allowing David two choices for each event, how would the outcome be affected? What we discover is the birth of a second David, with the *grace event* being the defining point, splitting the two.

Let me put it this way. If David had been my son I would have said to him, "You are more important to me than many sheep. Take care of yourself!" Indeed, it would have been common sense, from my way of looking at it, to do so. So let us say *my* David hides from the lion, protecting his own life. Here is where this hypothetical split would take place. We now have the potential for two types of David. Both are the same in all respects, except for the decision made when facing the lion. The first one who defeated the lion, and the second who protected his life. They have split at the grace event.

> Grace events represent the primary intention of God's grace through the Holy Spirit for the Christian—to work upon our lives until "Christ is formed" in us.

Let us assume that both Davids encounter a bear along their now separate time lines. We know the first David defeats the bear. On the other hand, there is good reason to believe the second David is going to protect his own life once again. *He has been formed by his choice at the previous grace event when he protected his life.* He will now act from within this new reality. The reckless but courageous victory over the lion never occurred for this David.

Now both Davids, each in his separate time line, meets Goliath. In each case the problems have grown more threatening, that is, from the lion to the bear, and now to Goliath—but God's grace has also increased (Rom. 5:20). Both Davids hear the taunts and curses of Goliath. Both are outraged, but, as history records, only the first accepts the challenge. The second stares, is angry, knows "someone" should do something, but stays put, as common sense dictates, behind the Israelite line where he is safe. He goes on to live a long full life, eventually inheriting his father's flock, marrying, and living to a ripe old age. Then he dies and is remembered by his family for a few generations.

The David that accepted the challenge will defeat Goliath, another encounter and victory over an even greater problem through God's grace. This turning point is the third defining moment in his life. He will become the most revered king Israel ever had, is loved and remembered by millions, and through his seed the Son of David, the true King and Savior of the world, is born.

There is no partiality with God (Eph. 6:9). He has no favorites. God is active *in this same way* in your life. His intention is for your personality to develop in a natural, even spontaneous, fashion. How does this happen? From the perspective of certain theories, there are stages to be worked through, problems to be understood, and emotional insights to gain. Sometimes such an approach is helpful. But as believers in God's Word we must remind ourselves that we have the mind of Christ (1 Cor. 2:16) and are growing into a more complete understanding of His thoughts.

The mind of Christ *is* God's perspective on everything! From His perspective, one consistent path for your life, from birth through to eternity, is foreknown (Rom. 8:29). Along that path, God has been, is, and shall be working *all* things for your ultimate good. He is forming you according to His intention and plan. You are being *transformed into His likeness* (2 Cor. 3:18). Therefore, the formation of your unique personality is actually a study in God's grace. It is His gracious Spirit that is developing you, with His intention to form you into a son or daughter of God.

CAN TWO WALK TOGETHER . . . ?

The one and only limitation to discovering the writing of the Spirit, or to learning and applying the lessons learned from our own grace events, is in not living our lives in agreement with God's intention. As the prophet Amos wrote, "Can two walk together, unless they are agreed?" (Amos 3:3). It seems simple enough, yet I believe it is the key to your personal growth and health.

If two are to walk together, they must be in agreement to walk at the same pace and to walk to the same place. Without this agreement they will drift apart. Inasmuch as you are in agreement with God's intention for you, you will recognize His activity in your life. You have your own path, or track, by which the Spirit is leading you. All too often we are not specifically aware of this guidance, yet a continuous flow of God's grace is forming each of us—and all who believe.

Be assured that the Spirit has begun this forming work within you and intends to complete it (Phil. 1:6). God's love, God Himself as He truly is, is being formed in you, and is forming you. He has pledged to carry His goal of formation through to its completion. His love is made complete in you (1 John 4:12).

> If two are to walk together, they must be in agreement to walk at the same pace and to walk to the same place.

A BLACK HOLE

Joshua, a distressed father, came to see me regarding his son David. The next day, David was being released from a psychiatric center, and his father needed help in dealing with this family crisis. David was twelve years old and severely overweight. His parents had divorced, and three weeks ago David moved in with his dad. Shortly after moving in, Joshua's new fiancée found a kitchen knife under David's pillow. A note was also discovered in his drawer that revealed some violent thoughts. Joshua was very concerned about this, as well as the music David was listening to that encouraged such brutal actions.

After a consultation with social services, David was taken to a local hospital, and from there he was referred to a psychiatric center. The staff psychiatrist recommended inpatient treatment. He was diagnosed as ADD and being in the midst of a major depression. The doctor prescribed Prozac for the depression and Ritalin for the ADD. He remained in the hospital for seventeen days, every day pleading for his father to take him home. Joshua was informed that David was most likely genetically predisposed to depression.

As I listened to this story I had the sensation of a great black hole spinning in space—drawing this family into its influence. With the best of intentions the mental health system had led this trusting family into a whirlpool of mental diseases and victimization. There is no doubt that David's behavior had been deteriorating. He felt angry, powerless, and hopeless. His world, like Humpty Dumpty, had broken to pieces, and he did not know how to put it back together again. Tragically, nothing within the present treatment approach was empowering him.

With children and teens, a large portion of the solution is right before us: to consistently and purposefully fill their emotional tank.

Indeed, the diagnosis and treatment made it clear that David was not responsible for his behavior. He had a disease. This medical observation remained so focused on David's problems that it blinded all involved from looking for family and personal strengths.

Though they were not a Christian family, I still believed God was already active in this household. Acting on this belief, I began to look for clues of His activity and preparation. I did not need to look far. Joshua was eager to do anything that would help. Nothing as serious as this incident with the knife and note had occurred previously, so we knew that there were many more times when David was *not* behaving in this way.

Joshua described how he recently sat with his son and, while hugging him, told him how much he loved him. I asked if this had helped David, and he said it had. In fact, it was a wonderful memory for him. As our discussion progressed, many strengths and capabilities were revealed in this concerned and loving father. I began to wonder what his son's strengths were. So far, no one else had explored David's capabilities or even discovered what he wanted.

I decided to talk with Joshua about David's "emotional tank." This is an extremely helpful concept developed by Dr. Ross Campbell. To illustrate it, I asked Joshua to consider his automobile. I asked him to imagine that his car's engine stalled, and he was stranded in traffic. After being towed, his car was examined by a mechanic in order to discover the problem. It was given a full tune-up, but still the engine would not start. The electrical system was checked, much of it being replaced, still without success. Finally, the engine was replaced. Even then the car would not start. Later on a different mechanic suggested checking to see if there was fuel in the tank. It was empty. Once the car's tank was filled, and the key was turned, the engine started right up.

We would all agree that the first mechanic had been ridiculously negligent. All that time and money to fix a car, when it was only out of gas.

We often follow the same procedures with our children that the mechanics did with the car. When we have problems with our children, we look for reasons that demand a great deal of expense and time. Sometimes the approach the experts recommend for fixing the problem becomes part of the problem! With children and teens, a large portion of the solution is right before us: to consistently and purposefully fill their emotional tank.

This tank is filled by loving and accepting eye contact, appropriate touching, and focused attention—more on this in a moment. I complimented Joshua for already doing some of this with his son. I encouraged him to deliberately continue his physical expressions of love, and to do so many times each day, since it was the one thing that had helped his son the most. I explained that it is possible to love our children, and yet they may not *feel* loved. Our goal must be for our children to *feel* loved, especially when they are in the midst, as David was, of such a confusing time in their lives. The emotional tank needs to be filled. When this tank is not filled, or is in need of filling, various problems begin to manifest. Focusing on correcting these problems is often a fruitless enterprise if the tank remains unfilled.

This reminds me of another "mental health" story. Ray Stedman told about a certain psychiatric center that had devised an unusual test to determine when patients were ready to go back into the world. They brought any candidates for release into a room where a tap was turned on and water was pouring out onto the floor. Next they handed the patient a mop and told him to mop up the water. If the patient had sense enough to turn off the tap before mopping up the water, he was ready to go out into society. But if, as in the case of many, he started mopping up the water while the tap was running, the doctors knew more treatment was needed.

The emotional tank is filled by loving and accepting eye contact, appropriate touching, and focused attention.

We may laugh, but isn't this what many of us are doing? First things first. First fill the tank, then use the mop to help correct the difficult situations. Or, like the story says, shut off the tap of past hurt, bitterness, and pain that a child who feels unloved experiences. Then, when we work on developing clearer communication we are not constantly losing ground.

David's dad said he would deliberately begin to do more of this when his son came home. I encouraged him to do so and make a mental note of what happened when he did. Then he was to repeat whatever helped David. I eventually saw Joshua, along with David, three more times. Without detailing the sessions, the end result was a child and family back on track. I continued to encourage them to do more of the things that they described to me as helpful and, like detectives, to try to catch each other doing these things. I complimented them on their successes and strengths, as well as helped them describe and stay on track toward their goals. Eventually, they became a team, the goal being to stay on track together.

Keep in mind that this entire story, from the hidden knife and notes, to being committed within the psychiatric hospital, were parts of an unfolding grace event and represented a turning point for this family. If Joshua had not reestablished emotional contact with his son at that time, a great opportunity would have been lost.

FILLING THE TANK

I remember as a child noticing my mom staring at me. I was a little curious as to what she was looking at, so I asked her. I have never forgotten her answer . . . "I'm loving you with my eyes," she replied. And so she was. More importantly, I *felt* loved by her. So today with my own children. I love them with my eyes, and they know it. Perhaps they wonder from time to time if Dad has "lost it," but they *feel* loved. It is *not* enough that I pay the bills and put a roof over their heads. I am responsible to prepare them to receive God's love. That is done when they can clearly recognize my love. So also, we spend time together, personal time when I am fully *there* for whichever child I am with, not thinking of the work I still need to do or the other responsibilities I may have at that moment. I'm so glad that our heavenly Father never treats us that way. He is always totally *there* for us—not with all the answers, but with Himself.

Also, whenever my kids walk past me or are near me, I reach out and make physical contact with them, touching them in one way or another—a quick shoulder rub, a soft pat on their cheeks, or just leaning against them, always appropriate touching, of course. I also initiated something called the thirty-second hug— simply a hug that lasts thirty seconds. I discovered that the first ten seconds were functional, the second ten seconds revealed resignation, but the third ten seconds were when two souls touched, and we knew that we were not alone. When I hug my kids for thirty seconds, we, at that moment, become united in something bigger than both of us—the love of God. Even my teenage sons and preteen daughter have not fully outgrown this. I suppose that day will come, but I pray it will then be replaced as they love their children and spouses in the same way.

Now is the time to love and be loved. *Today* is the day to fill the emotional tank. For God says, "In the time of my favor I heard you, and in the day of salvation I helped you. I tell you, now is the time of God's favor, now is the day of salvation" (2 Cor. 6:2). Each moment reveals more of God's grace—if we will act on that which has already been given. Your life has been touched by God.

Key Points and Action Steps for Personal Application

KEY POINT 1

When you assume God's presence is in your life, you begin to look for clues of His activity. Two such clues are the writing of the Spirit and grace events. The story of your life is so interwoven with God's Spirit that you could view your very life as the writing of the Spirit. God has been closer to you than your very breath, but you may not have appreciated His presence. Also, you are growing *in* grace, being rewritten through numerous encounters *with* God's grace. These grace events reveal past problems, successfully encountered, that you can utilize to prepare yourself for present and future challenges. Each one reveals God's grace in the concrete issues of your life—thus serving as turning points.

➤ Action Step 1

- In your notebook, write down some of your most memorable life experiences—challenges large and small—that you successfully handled. Start with your childhood. Take plenty of time with the exercise. When you are finished, look over what you have written and see if you can highlight the grace events that helped to develop the stronger and more compassionate aspects of your personality. What have you have discovered? Write it down.
- Look also for the writing of the Spirit, the times when you can recognize that God entered the story of your life in a more direct fashion. What happened specifically? Again, summarize what you found and write it down.

- Now you want to apply what you have learned regarding your own grace events and the writing of the Spirit in your life. How can you use this information with your present goals regarding your home, family, work, education, and church?
- What will you be doing when you are using more of your strengths that God has woven into your life through specific experiences? Begin to do a little of this in a deliberate way.

KEY POINT 2

God's deliberate intention is for past, present, and future difficulties to accomplish good. This is primarily true for those who seek to live according to His designed purpose. This design is God's plan to form you and to help you feel loved as you recognize that you are not alone.

➤ Action Step 2

- On the scale below, where ten means your family feels loved by you, and one means they are often running on an empty tank, where would you say they are right now?

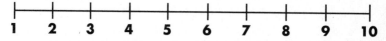

- Today, make a conscious decision to act toward your loved ones in a new way. "Love them with your eyes." Also, offer brief shoulder rubs, softly touch their cheeks, or just lean close to them. Try initiating something like my thirty-second hugs so your loved ones *feel* loved and *know* they are not alone in life's journey. Also, spend individual time with each one as often as possible so you can more intentionally focus your attention upon them, listening to them, and loving them more deliberately—just as God loves you. What will you be doing differently at the next highest number on the scale? Be specific.

chapter seven

Get Involved! It's Your Life

I've never met a person, I don't care what his condition, in whom I could not see possibilities. I don't care how much a man may consider himself a failure, I believe in him, for he can change the thing that is wrong in his life any time he is ready and prepared to do it. Whenever he develops the desire, he can take away from his life the thing that is defeating it. The capacity for reformation and change lies within.

PRESTON BRADLEY

One does not discover new lands without consenting to lose sight of the shore for a very long time.

ANDRÉ GIDE

In my opinion, Jesus' most scathing denunciation to the religious leaders of His day was that they were not willing to believe. "If you are the Christ," they said, "tell us." Jesus answered, "If I tell you, *you will not* believe me . . ." (Luke 22:67, italics added). Even through His tears He proclaimed the hardness of their hearts: "How often I have longed to gather your children together . . . but *you were not willing*" (Matt. 23:37, italics added). So also with us today. God shows no partiality. He feels as strongly about this today as He did with the religious leaders 2000 years ago. Being willing is the most important prerequisite to spiritual growth. After all, it is your life—therefore it is *your* responsibility.

Yet, as you get more fully involved in your own development as a human being, in the development of your spiritual growth, you will begin to see God's hand more clearly as He is forming you—since God has always been completely involved in your life. But, why do we so often fall short in this most crucial area? Again, we get stuck. We reach the end of our resources, our ability to see, and are unable to recognize the hand of God, or the writing of the Spirit in our own lives. Does this mean we are abandoned by God? Of course not. What it means is we are not seeing what God is doing because our mind, both spiritually and physically, has not yet developed to the point that we can see. Our perceptions fail us, but not God's intention for our lives. His intention remains the same.

GO ASK ALICE

When it comes to God's intention, our *willingness* to learn is everything. Through our willingness we become teachable. Consider Alice ... Alice from Wonderland, that is. Remember when she met the caterpillar in the cartoon version of the story? He was blowing wonderful smoke rings that would spell out the question, "Who are you?" Alice answered reasonably, "I'm Alice." Then the caterpillar repeated the question in the smoke

> When it comes to God's intention, our willingness to learn is everything. Through our willingness we become teachable.

rings. Once again Alice's answer remained the same. Somehow her responses were insufficient. What was missing? I believe Alice was more than what she knew herself to be—more than she was aware of. She did not truly see herself.

Instead, she could have said something like what the apostle John once said: "Dear friends, now we are children of God, and *what we will be has not yet been made known.* But we know that when he appears, we shall be like him, for we shall see him as he is" (1 John 3:2, italics added). That would have shut up that pesky caterpillar! The term "made known" is from a Greek word that means to render apparent or to appear—to see. We do not yet *see* what we shall be, but we know we shall be like Jesus Christ. Therefore, the apostle John was fully willing and in agreement with God's intention for him. This informed all the "roles" he played.

Many of us think we *are* the roles we play. This was Alice's error. She saw herself as Alice, a little girl. Think of the roles you play. Perhaps you are a mom or dad, a brother or sister, a son or daughter, a grandson or granddaughter, a coworker, boss, neighbor, aunt or uncle, nephew or niece. You have various roles within your church, as a follower of Christ, and many more in other areas of life. But what *informs* these roles? What is the glue that holds them all together?

I have counseled women whose children are grown and gone, leaving Mom without a purpose. Men have been so defined by their jobs that at retirement they lose who they are—not really knowing what is wrong. But, when we become an active participant in our own lives, we begin to deliberately watch and remain in agreement with God's intention as it unfolds "spontaneously." We realize that, with our existence as God's child, the whole is greater than the sum of its parts. That is, you are more than the roles you play. Yet, in God each role is both serving others and *forming you.* I can hear the still, small voice ever so clearly in my spirit during the various issues and difficulties of life. He is saying, "Pay attention, and you will learn who you are—you will learn to see!"

This is not meant to be mystical or even deeply spiritual. Rather, it is supremely practical. We cannot help but grow in Christ if we will but pay attention and remain willing to learn.

OXYGEN

If you have had occasion to fly you may have noticed that the flight attendants always utilize a checklist in going over safety instructions with the passengers before takeoff. One of the points checked off is the use of the oxygen mask. Personally, I always get a little nervous when they demonstrate how it will drop out of the overhead at just the right moment if the plane depressurizes. I would rather not hear about that right as the plane is leaving the ground!

Have you ever observed how the attendant will instruct parents to place the mask over their faces before trying to place the mask on their children? I know if I were traveling with my children, I would be tempted to ignore this procedure. But, I would ignore it at my own peril, and thus endanger my children. Of course, we need to take care of our own oxygen before we can help our children—or anyone else for that matter. If we pass out there will be no one to save our child. So also, in life.

Isn't it interesting that we have to "get involved" in our own safety before we can care for the safety of others—whether it be family, friends, or strangers. What is true in the sky is certainly true on the ground. We have to become actively involved in our own safety, our own growing and becoming, before we can truly be supportive of others. We cannot give what we do not have. We must become willing to see what God is doing in our lives, each day, in order to be trained by Him and apply these lessons to our various roles and responsibilities.

> We have to "get involved" in our own safety, before we can care for the safety of others.

WAX ON, WAX OFF

Do you remember *The Karate Kid*? In this movie a young man is confronted by bullies. He is beaten and ridiculed but saved at the last moment by a mysterious warrior. This "warrior" turns out to be a simple, elderly man, who is highly disciplined in the art of karate. Of course, the youngster becomes his student, learning from the master the ways of this discipline. Full of enthusiasm, he shows up for his first lesson. He is deeply disappointed though, when he is instructed to wax the master's old car. He is taught to put the wax on with one motion and take the wax off with the opposite motion. His disillusionment increases when he discovers that there are many more old cars to wax. He wants to give up. Where is the adventure? He wants to learn *fast* so he can take his vengeance on those bullies. Again, the master points him back to the dull old cars. Wax on, wax off!

> If we are not willing, we cannot learn—even though the lessons are clearly all around us.

Finally he gives in, not truly understanding but willing to trust. Some grumbling and soreness later, he is no closer than he was in the beginning to learning karate. At least that is his perception. He had not yet seen the master's *intention*. Finally, he discovers that he has actually learned some essential skills, even though he was not fully aware of being trained. His experience and work were not in vain. More importantly, now that he sees, he is able to learn the heart of his master—and the anger is removed from his hands.

Does it seem that your days are full of "wax on, wax off"? We do not see the purpose, even though the Creator of our eyes has given us the ability to *see*. We want to learn fast, so we can deal with the "bullies" in our lives. Yet, these same "bullies" drive us to the only true Master, and He begins to show us that our training is already in progress—if we would but open our eyes. "What, more wax, Lord?" If we are not willing . . . we cannot learn—even though the lessons of life are clearly and continually all around us.

So what is stopping us? Well, if we are not in a *willing* position with God, there are at least two other positions we may be in. Either we are *blaming* or we are simply *attending,* not really paying attention. Let's look at all three.

POSITIONS

Question: How many counselors does it take to screw in a lightbulb?

Answer: Just one, but the lightbulb has to be willing.

When we are in a "willing" position we tend to have a clearer view of the problems we face. The problem may be about someone else or about ourselves, but we can clearly visualize the situation, and we are ready to do something about it. We are willing to do something different because what we are presently doing is not working.

Unfortunately, we all too often find ourselves in what I call a "blaming" position. When we are blaming we have a great deal of information about a problem that *someone else* has, but we do not see ourselves as part of the solution. Perhaps you view yourself as a victim of your situation or your past. Or you have been told by another counselor that you have a psychiatric disorder or disease. Either way, any potential solution seems to reside beyond you. A woman may, for example, talk with her pastor about a problem regarding her husband or child. If she is in a blaming position, she knows a great deal about the situation and can help the pastor better understand it. But what she wants is for *the other person* to be different. The husband or child is defined *as* the problem. When we are in such a position we view ourselves as waiting helplessly for something or someone to change. In marriage it may seem that the spouse must change before the relationship can improve—thus the marriage is stuck.

Every so often we find ourselves simply "attending"—not really paying attention. Like window-shoppers, we are not ready or willing to make a purchase. In fact, through this third possible position we may actually be digging in our heels, unwilling to see ourselves in any way as part of the solution. Others may feel you need some help, but you have no desire to enter in.

WHERE ARE YOU?

Based on these definitions, where are you today? Clearly, when we are willing to seek a new approach to old problems, we have a greater possibility of progress. If nothing else, we will at least see clearly what we can do, and in doing it achieve the satisfaction that comes from having done all we can. Consider for a moment a scale of one to ten. On this scale a ten means with God's help, you will do whatever is necessary to solve the problems you are facing at the present time. At the bottom of the scale a one means you will sit and wait for something to happen. On this scale where would you put yourself today? . . . If your number is lower than expected, you may want to examine your own willingness to truly become a full partner in God's intention for your life.

> When we are blaming we have a great deal of information about a problem someone else has, but we do not see ourselves as part of the solution.

At such times not only are we stuck, but we are blaming others for our being stuck. We are like Adam crying out toward God, "The woman you put here with me—she gave me some fruit from the tree, and I ate it" (Gen. 3:12). "Not only is it not my fault," Adam was insisting, "but it's her fault and Your fault."

I once reminded a middle-aged man who came to me for counseling that he had great strength and power in Christ—but that he could all too easily give it away. To illustrate this point I asked him to write the word "power" on the back of a small business card. Then we also dis-cussed wisdom—defining it not as knowing what to do ultimately, but knowing what to do next. I asked him to draw a line under the word "power" and write the word "wis-dom." I invited him to place the card in his pocket and to remove it

> As soon as we begin to blame, we just as quickly give away our power and strength in Jesus Christ, and with it our wisdom to know what to do next!

only when he began to blame anyone—including himself—for anything. He was to take out the card and give it away to that person. In so doing he was acknowledging the truth behind his actions, for as soon as we begin to blame, we just as quickly give away our power and strength in Jesus Christ, and with it our wisdom to know what to do next! Although the card may go to the individual, our power is actually given up to the Enemy of our souls.

THE STATUE OF RESPONSIBILITY

It has been said that when America placed the Statue of Liberty on the east coast, we should have also placed a "Statue of Respon-sibility" on the west coast. All freedom comes with a price: responsibility. We allow our children the *freedom* to cross the street, when they are old enough to accept the *responsibility* to look both ways. So also, we are made free in Jesus (John 8:32). Yet, this freedom also brings with it a new responsibility. We are free to develop the mind and thoughts of Christ in any difficult situation. Interestingly, in so doing our decisions actually form our developing character and integrity. But, every time we blame, we step away from the truth, denying our responsibility, and los-ing our freedom—for only truth can make us free.

THE DOORKNOB

During a conference where I was a presenter on the topic of solution-focused pastoral counseling, I attempted to illustrate the cardinal fact regarding truth: truth works. I walked over to a closed door and questioned aloud what I would do if I had never seen a door before. I knew that I could use it to leave the room, and for purposes of the illustration, I needed to leave the room, but I wouldn't know how. In other words, I was *stuck* on the wrong side of the door. When I approached it, I tried pushing the doorknob like a big button, to no avail. Then I tried pulling on the coat hook. Certainly it was a lever that would open the door. Nothing worked. Finally, I tried turning the knob, and . . . the door opened.

The only way for me to get unstuck and through the door to the other side was to know the truth of the door, that is, to turn the doorknob. Once done, it opened. It had to! So also with the truth of God's Word—which is the mind of Christ. As we willingly come into agreement with the intention of God's Word, our minds are formed by truth. And truth works! We begin to see options and solutions where none seemed to exist. As we move forward into these solutions our competence grows and we become confident enough to look back at old hurts and pains, reaching backward to reclaim the years that seemed forever lost. Again, I believe that this is what God meant when He spoke through the prophet Joel saying, "I will restore to you the years that the swarming locust has eaten" (Joel 2:25 NKJV).

> **As we willingly come into agreement with the intention of God's Word, our minds are formed by truth. And truth works!**

HOW ABOUT YOU?

So let us say that you are in a situation where you have come to a "door" in your life, and you cannot get to the other side. Can you gauge your willingness to go through the door, once the truth of it is determined? Of course the truth is found in God's intention for you. His intention is for you to utilize your freedom in Christ in a responsible way. That must mean that you now become willing to do all that *you* can do, without looking for others to change first.

Where are you on the scale? Remember, on this scale a ten means that, with God's help, you will do anything to solve the problems you are facing at the present time. At the bottom of the scale, a one means you will sit and wait for something to happen. Let us say you are a four. What will you be doing differently when you are a five? If a seven, what will you be doing differently when you are an eight? What are *you* willing to do to move forward in your life? Now think of this in a specific way. What *exactly* will you do first? What next?

Take a moment to write down what the Holy Spirit is saying to you. Then, ask yourself, "What will I be doing differently?" "What will my family and friends notice that is different about me when I'm doing this?" "What will I observe about them as they react to me doing this?" "What will they see me doing that is different?" "How will I do it that way more often?" Questions like these honor God in that they quickly bring us into agreement with the Holy Spirit, who is teaching us to move forward one step at a time, not wait for others to make the first move.

So if you have anger in your heart toward anyone, what should you do? Well, what are you willing to do? It's your life, how will you choose to live it? Will you wait for the other person to change? You may wait a long time. And all the while that anger is growing roots, becoming bitterness, resentment, and unforgiveness. Are you waiting for your feelings to change? Again, you may be waiting a long time. Remember, those feelings are flowing directly from *your* thoughts and actions—so always seek to act your way into a new feeling, rather than trying to feel your way into a new action. Also, although the anger was not sin (Eph. 4:26), the bitterness and resentment is. So what can you do? Actually, everything Jesus can do—which is quite enough.

> **The Holy Spirit is teaching us to move forward one step at a time, not waiting for others to make the first move.**

First you acknowledge that it is *your* anger. After all, it is coming from *your* brain. Remember that everything you are feeling is from *your* neural pathways. If you are stuck in anger and unforgiveness, it is because you have not yet seen the truth of the "doorknob." You are seeing only the "old hag" or the "young woman," but you are not seeing yet as Jesus sees. You will, though, if you are willing. Wax on, wax off! You see, if it is *your* anger, *you* have final say as to what to do with it. *You* are in control! Now what? Instead of reacting to the emotion of anger, you allow the anger to remind you of your responsibility to demonstrate the mind of Christ. You stop, take a few breaths, and offer a prayer of thanksgiving to God, and then *decide* what to do with *your* anger.

What exactly will you do first? Here's what I do. I remind myself that it is probably due to *my* goal being blocked or *my* feelings being hurt that I am angry. So I ask myself, "What was my goal? How has my ego been threatened, thus hurting my feelings?" If I can truthfully admit these to myself, I can swiftly discover the origin of my anger. Then, as honestly as I can, I remind myself that my goal is not God's goal for that situation or relationship. My ego is threatened and my feelings are hurt *primarily* because my goal is not in agreement with God's goal. I believe the foundational truth here is that God's goal is to teach me through this situation, helping me continue the process of mastering my anger. I do not believe He is concerned at that moment with who is right and who is wrong, or whether I get my way, or whether I've been heard. If I refuse this lesson, I have chosen to believe that my way is better than God's, that is, I have chosen to act with boastful pride. "Pride only breeds quarrels, but wisdom is found in those who take advice" (Prov. 13:10). When I am involved in a quarrel or an argument, I am only demonstrating my pride—and that I am a poor student.

What next? I will choose to pray for those who mistreat me (Luke 6:28). (That does not mean praying to God to bless them with a brick!) When we follow Jesus in this action we actually break the stranglehold the anger had on us. We sever the chain that was keeping us stuck in prison. Then what? I will do good to those who hate me (Luke 6:27).

Now you are ready to write down what the Holy Spirit is saying to you. "What will I be doing differently?" I will treat this person as one whom I have prayed for, and as one for whom Jesus died. "What will my family and friends notice that is different about me when I'm doing this?" They will hear me saying kind things about this individual. I will seek ways to encourage this person whenever possible. "What will I observe about this person as he or she reacts to me doing this?" This is fascinating. Always observe what happens when you act with the mind of Christ. You will see healing take place right

Be both verbally and non-verbally open and caring—as if the relationship is healthy already.

before your eyes, first in your spirit, then in the relationship. "What will this individual see me doing that is different?" I will be both verbally and nonverbally open and caring—as if the relationship is healthy already.

Then the truly mysterious and marvelous happens. My feelings actually change. I care about this person. Why? Because Jesus did first, and His mind is being formed in me . . . literally. So also for you. Are you struggling in areas of anger or unforgiveness? Perhaps it is toward a spouse or parent. Maybe it is toward a fellow worker or church member. You have prayed about it, but nothing has changed. Why? Because you prayed about *it*, not for the *person*. The mind of Christ is *doing*, not simply thinking or talking about the situation. As you *act*, your feelings will change. Are you willing?

Key Points and Action Steps for Personal Application

KEY POINT 1

Being willing to learn is your most important prerequisite to spiritual growth. It is your *life, so it is* your *responsibility.* When it comes to God's design for your life, your willingness to learn is everything. Without it you cannot learn—even though the lessons from God are clearly and continually all around you. Through your willingness you become teachable. When your will is daily turned over to God, each "role" you play not only serves other people, but it forms you. It is as if God is saying, "Pay attention, and you will learn who you are."

➤ Action Step 1

- Get a small business card and write the word "power" on the back. Now, draw a line under the word "power" and write the word "wisdom." Keep this card in your pocket, and remove it only when you begin to blame anyone for anything. Then, take out the card and imagine yourself giving it away to that person you are blaming. Remind yourself through this action that you are beginning to give away your power and strength in Jesus Christ—and with it your wisdom to know what to do next. Write down what you noticed about yourself and others when you did this.

- You can stop blaming by seeing this person and situation as a part of your personal education. Then you will assume your responsibility to learn from God. As you do this, you will reclaim the card and put it back in your pocket. Again, write down what you noticed when you did this. How did the interaction change? Do more of what works.

KEY POINT 2

God has made you to be free to develop the mind and thoughts of Christ in any difficult situation. In so doing your decisions will correctly form your character and strengthen your integrity. Since you cannot give to others what you do not have, your willingness to take full responsibility to be trained by God's Spirit is essential in helping you apply God's specific lessons to your various situations.

➤ Action Step 2

- On the following scale, where ten means with God's help you will do whatever is necessary to solve the problems you are facing at the present time, and one means you will sit and wait for something to happen, where would you put yourself today?

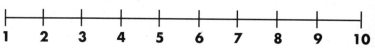

- When you are more willing to do whatever is necessary to solve your problems, what will be the first thing you will need to do?
- What will you be doing differently when you are at the next number? What exactly will you do first? What next? Take a moment to write down what the Holy Spirit is saying to you.
- What will your family and friends notice that is different about you when you are doing this?
- What will you observe about them as they react to you doing this?
- What will they see you doing that is different?
- How will you do it that way more often?

chapter eight

Problem Solved? Now What?

> The Bible does not simply address the modern world; it wants to create a whole new world that cannot be seen without conversion.
>
> WILLIAM WILLIMON

Did you ever notice when you were a child that your mom could be yelling at you, and then the phone would ring and she could answer it calmly? It was truly astonishing. One moment, red in the face and shouting, "You wait until your father comes home!" Then, [ring] ... "Hellooo" ... as sweet as can be. How is it that she could be shouting one moment and calm the next? Worse than that, how is it that we who are now parents have found this same ability within ourselves? It never ceases to amaze me. Our children are as bewildered as we were. I think part of the answer is that the immediate problem with our children is not all there is to life—as much as it may seem to be at the moment. The phone shows us that this is not the case. We can shift in our emotions quite quickly when we need to. How we do that is important to creating solutions.

A DEPRESSED WOMAN

Recently, a woman came to me for counseling, saying she was "clinically" depressed. (I suppose when the word "clinically" precedes the word "depressed" the situation is very, very, bad!) All the "symptoms" were evident. She had currently been feeling down most of the time—somewhat empty inside. She was having difficulty sleeping and felt fatigued often. To make things worse, her ability to concentrate had been affected, and she had lost interest in most activities. I asked her the following question: "Many times between calling for an appointment and the first counseling session, people already notice some improvement—something seems a little different. What have you noticed?" Her response was not unusual. She could find little that was improved.

She did happen to mention that she had rented a movie the night before and that she enjoyed it. We talked about the movie for a little while, and then I asked her if she had felt depressed while she was watching it. She looked at me, her jaw dropped, and she replied that she had not. I wondered out loud how that could be, if she were "clinically" depressed. Her honest response was that the movie took her mind off of her depression. So I asked, "Is it unusual for you to do this, that is, get your mind off of the depression?" She replied that she was able to do it from time to time. At this point I was getting curious, so I asked, "What will you have to continue to do to get that to happen more often?" She then began to describe for me things she would need to do to get her mind off her depression.

The list grew as we talked, until at last I suggested that she do some of these things in a very deliberate fashion. She was also to notice what happened when she did so, so she could tell me what she observed and how others reacted to her. She agreed. The next time we spoke she indicated that life was beginning to "work" again. She went on to tell me about the changes she had made and how her family and friends had responded to her increased activity, and how she was enjoying their response. "Are these the sort of changes you would like to continue to have happen?" I asked. Her reply was an enthusiastic yes.

From that time on she slowly, step by step, walked her way out from under the weight of depression. How? She did so by getting unstuck and back on track. As she developed greater competence and increased activity, she saw that she actually felt better

> We can shift in our emotions quite quickly when we need to. How we do that is important to creating solutions.

the more she entered back into her life. It wasn't long before her emotions followed suit.

WHAT DO YOU WANT?

What is it that you really want? Think about it. If you are anything like many of those who come to me for counseling, you spend much of your time thinking about and discussing what you *do not want*. You may find yourself rehearsing your problems again and again in your thoughts, or talking them over with others. Unfortunately, as you focus on your problems in this way, you are inadvertently reinforcing them. I certainly understand the need to have someone who will listen to you when you are hurting emotionally. At times we all need a sympathetic ear, someone who can offer some encouragement. Yet, when we overly indulge in talking about our problems the result is often greater frustration—not only for ourselves but for those who are kind enough to listen to us.

Instead, you could ask yourself, *What has God already placed in my life that is working?* and *Can I do more of that on purpose?* We all too often want to discuss what is wrong and what is not working. Since we are all unique, it becomes increasingly difficult to obtain agreement on what is wrong, or even on what the problem is. Everyone has a different opinion. When you look for what *is* working and what you would like to see continue, it is possible to reach some agreement with others. Again, this assumes that God is actively engaged in your life.

> If what you are doing is not working, it is time to try something new. You cannot dig yourself out of a hole by continuing to dig deeper.

What can you do that is different? If what you are doing is not working, it is time to try something new. You cannot dig yourself out of a hole by continuing to dig deeper. God is always intentionally doing a "new thing" in our lives. His working allows you too to do a "new thing"; your behavior need not be locked into old patterns and choices. Because of this direct intention of the Spirit, each moment and choice is saturated with significance. Since our heavenly Father is the author of all true originality, He can break into our lives and help us do a completely new thing.

Doing something new is the real trademark of our heavenly Father. But, do we *see* this new approach or option when it appears? Insanity is doing the same thing again and again . . . and expecting different results! I remember when my children were little I would playfully and gently box them with their own hands. They would laugh and laugh at the absurdity of being beaten up by themselves in this silly fashion. But when Satan does it to us, there is nothing funny about it. We beat ourselves up, doing the same thing again and again, yet the Enemy is moving our arms and hands. Friend . . . if it's not working, stop doing it!

What if you could take a vacation from your problems? Now remember, the problem nearly always begins outside of you. The only way it gets within you is by how you react to it. Imagine for a moment that you really *are* on vacation. Now that you are away from the problem, what is differ-ent? That is, what is different when the problem is not happening? Hard to imagine? Then let's try something else. Let us say that

> **Insanity is doing the same thing again and again . . . and expecting different results!**

tonight, while you are sleeping, a miracle takes place, and the problems you are wrestling with are solved. But, as I said, you were sleeping—so you are not aware that this miracle has occurred. Tomorrow morning when you get out of bed, what will you notice that will tell you that this miracle has happened?[1]

THE LOTTO WINNER

One fellow who was seeing me due to his feelings of anxiety, responded to this question by saying, "I will have won the Lotto!" Wise guy! Yet, it was an enthusiastic answer, so I asked him, "What will be different when you win the Lotto?" "Well, my problems would be gone, that's for sure," he replied. "Tell me more about that," I asked curiously. He then proceeded to tell me

[1] Adapted from a question presented by Steve de Shazer in *Clues: Investigating Solutions in Brief Therapy* (New York: W. W. Norton, 1988).

all the things he would be doing if he were rich. It was amazing how his disposition changed as he described his newfound wealth.

Yet, the things he described were all things he could have been doing without the wealth. He could see himself arguing less with his children. He was also calmer on the road in traffic and on the job with coworkers. He was more relaxed when his children were playing Little League baseball. Somehow whether they won or lost was not as important anymore. He just wanted them

> "I know the plans I have for you, . . . plans to prosper you and not to harm you, plans to give you hope and a future" (Jer. 29:11).

to have a good time. His presentations for his bosses were not nearly as stressful, since he was not so dependent on their approval. Best of all, he could *see* a much-improved relationship with his wife. He discovered that he was much more patient and understanding.

I decided to discuss this miracle more on the basis of his faith in God, than in the lottery. So, we read together the prophet Jeremiah's words. Remember, God spoke through him, saying, "I know the plans I have for you, . . . plans to *prosper* you and not to harm you, plans to give you hope and a future" (Jer. 29:11, italics added). I asked whether it would also be a miracle day when he could clearly recognize his prosperity was secure in God, not just financially through the Lotto. He said it would be. I then suggested that he let tomorrow be a miracle day, where God had prospered him beyond anything he could truly appreciate.

With this in view, I asked him, "On a scale of one to ten, with ten being a miracle day, and one being an ordinary day, where would you say you are today?" His answer was a two. I recommended that he deliberately be a three in his behaviors, as on a miracle day, and carefully observe what happens, including other people's responses. When we next met he *had* noticed a difference—especially at work. His bosses responded to his calmer presentation with increased attentiveness and appreciation. The result was that his normally anxious demeanor was more relaxed. "I could get used to this," was his response to me. His wife also noticed, and as he deliberately did more and more of the "miracle," both of them could see the difference.

THE HAND IN FRONT OF YOUR FACE

Sometimes our problems feel so overwhelming that they become all we can see. We get up in the morning worrying about our problems, we think about them throughout the day, and we have them on our minds when we go to sleep at night. No wonder our relationships are strained and our bodies weakened! Again, we are stuck, unable to see the next step. Yet, God already sees it, and His intention is to allow it to spontaneously unfold, as we keep our minds stayed on Him.

Try this helpful illustration of this dilemma. After you have read this paragraph, put down the book and place your hand about two inches away from the front of your face, covering your view. Your hand represents the problems you are facing. Now slowly straighten your arm. As you can see, your view of your hand (your problems) changes dramatically when you look at it from a distance. Primarily the problem was the closeness of your hand to your face. Also, you can see far more of the room— which in this case represents other options and possibilities. The problems do not seem so overwhelming when viewed at "arm's length." Unfortunately, we all too often fail to do this until relationships and physical health have already deteriorated. Yet, that very decline should be a sign to us to try something different—if we were only paying attention.

A CREEPY GUY

In my book on solution-focused counseling I tell a story about a time I was feeling pretty depressed. I was in college and my roommate talked me into getting up and going out on the campus. Many of the students were dressing up because it was Halloween. Although we did not observe this holiday as such, it gave us an excuse to unwind and get silly. My roommate gave me a rubber mask of an old man, as well as his baggy overalls and large boots. Since he was well over six feet tall, my much smaller frame was dwarfed in his clothing. But, when I put it all on I was astonished at my change in personality.

My new "persona" grew as the evening progressed. I spent the rest of the evening walking around the campus crooked and stooped over, dragging one foot, and mumbling. All night my fellow students were trying to figure out who I was. They had such a hard time because this old man was so unlike me. In a sense, I became that crooked old man for an evening. I also began to follow a cute, young female student around the campus. Every time she turned around, there I was, creeping up behind her, with the emphasis on creep! I was quite comfortable in my alternate identity. (By the way, this cute, young student and I have been married for twenty years now.)

What happened? I took my focus off of my problem of feeling depressed, and my emotions followed. Of course, we must not hide behind "masks" to avoid our problems. It is God who is slowly, painstakingly removing our masks. But, the principle is true. For a few hours that night I felt fine. Why? Because what I was doing was working better than what I had been doing. Rather than withdrawing, I reengaged. Without realizing it, I acted as if the problems that were getting me down were solved—and the result was a momentary change in emotion. I was also later able to use my renewed energy to tackle some of the problems that were affecting me, and thereby raise my level of confidence.

> Your perceptions are lying to you—and the Enemy of your soul is the author of this lie.

Unfortunately, it is when we are struggling that we need our strength and determination the most. Of course, this is usually when they are both most lacking. Thank God, it is when we are weak, that we are truly strong! (2 Cor. 12:10). The Holy Spirit also led the apostle Paul to write, "Let God be true, and every man a liar" (Rom. 3:4). God says you are truly strong *when* you are at your weakest. Yet, your perceptions tell you this is not true. Let me say this as boldly and biblically as I can: Your perceptions are lying to you, and the Enemy of your soul is the author of this lie.

You are at a crossroads in your life—a grace event. The choices you make at such times form who you become. Consider the Chinese word *weichi*, which means "crisis." *Wei* means "danger" and, of course, there is great danger in a crisis. But *chi* means "opportunity." In the midst of a crisis there is both danger *and* opportunity. It is your responsibility—and God's intention—for you to find and choose the opportunity side. You are going to be formed by your decisions at the crossroads. It is up to you to determine how you are going to mature in Christ.

PROBLEM SOLVED? NOW WHAT?

Imagine for a moment what you will be doing when the problems that you are dealing with are solved. Seek to create an "observing" approach to life, rather than a "reacting" one. Ask yourself the following questions: *What will I be doing instead of the problems? How exactly will I be doing this?* and *As I continue to do these things, will I see myself as being on track?* In this way you will be on your way to creating real solutions—ones that lie within your hands to accomplish. These solutions may not fix everyone else's problems, but you will be at your very best so that you can be supportive to those around you—without taking on the responsibility for their personal problems.

> Seek to create an "observing" approach to life rather than a "reacting" one.

Just as a rising tide lifts all the ships in the harbor, so also greater competence lifts all your other roles and responsibilities to a higher level—with your emotions following.

Key Points and Action Steps for Personal Application

KEY POINT 1

Finding exceptions to your present problems will help you to rediscover strengths and capabilities. Often it seems as though your problems are happening all of the time. But there are always exceptions to those times. These are important to recognize if you are to solve your problem.

➤ Action Step 1a

(Please note that there are two different sets of questions for completion of this action step. Therefore, you will not be answering all the questions.)

- This week, notice what is different about the times when a problem is not happening—the exceptions. Again, imagine that you were on videotape. What would you see? Describe these "exceptions" that you are seeing in your video imagination as descriptively as you can. Be patient with this exercise. Give it an entire week to develop, writing down what you notice each day. The following questions will guide you through the week.
- What do you notice different about yourself during these times?
- How often do these "exceptions" occur?
- What is happening right before and right after these times?
- Put your responses to the above questions in one descriptive summary.
- Pick out the times that these exceptions were deliberate on your part. That is, when did they reveal deliberate actions you took, apart from anyone else's help, to improve the situation? List these. (If you have not noticed any times the exceptions were *deliberate,* then stop here and proceed to "Action Step 1b" on page 130.)
- Will you be satisfied and feel that your problem would be solved if these things happened more often?
- After a full week of answering the above questions, keep a record each day for one more week of what is different during these "exceptional" times. List the things you notice that you believe made a difference during such times.
- Next week summarize what you have noticed that is different or better since you began paying attention to exceptions. Look back over your notes for each day and reflect on anything that you observed that was better or different. What have you noticed that you want to have continue to happen?

- What do you notice that is different about the times the problem does not happen?
- What did others notice?
- What will need to happen in order for these "exceptions" to happen more often? Please be specific.
- In what ways have these changes helped you feel better about yourself?
- What will you need to keep doing to stay on track?
- Describe the difference you have noticed between this week and last week. What progress have you observed?
- List three things that you will do to keep this progress going. Remember, do more of what is working.

➤ **Action Step 1b**

(Skip this exercise if you completed Action Step 1a for this chapter.)

- Suppose that tonight, while you are sleeping, a miracle takes place, and the problems you are wrestling with are solved. But, as I said, you were sleeping—so you are not aware that this miracle has occurred. Tomorrow morning when you get out of bed, what will you notice that will tell you that this miracle has happened? Write out your response as fully and descriptively as possible in your notebook.
- Review your answer and look for any words such as "can't," "wouldn't," "couldn't," "won't," and "shouldn't." For example, if you said that you wouldn't be fighting with your spouse, ask yourself what you will be doing instead. Or, if you said you wouldn't be eating so much, ask yourself what you will be doing instead.
- Again, review what you have now written and ask yourself what you will be doing differently on this miracle day. Describe what is different about you.
- On the following scale, with ten being the miracle day you have described, and one being an ordinary day, where would you say you are today?

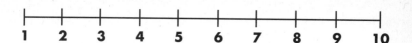

- When you move up to the next number, what deliberate actions will you be taking, apart from anyone else's help, to improve the situation? List three specific actions you identified.
- This week, pay attention to the times you are doing these things and write down what you observe that is different as you do so. Next week, summarize what you have noticed that is different or better since you began paying attention to what you are doing on miracle days. Look back over your notes for each day and reflect on anything that you observed that was better or different.
- What have you noticed that you want to have continue to happen?
- What do you notice that is different about the times the problem does not happen?
- What did others notice?
- What will need to happen in order for these "miracles" to happen more often? Please be specific.
- In what ways have these changes helped you feel better about yourself?
- What will you need to keep doing to stay on track?
- Describe the difference you have noticed between this week and last week. What progress have you observed? List three things that you will do to keep this progress going. Remember, do more of what is working.

KEY POINT 2

Emotions change quickly. Our reaction to a problem has the greatest impact on our experience of the problem. Your most difficult experiences in life represent drastic and abrupt changes. In the midst of any crisis there is both danger and opportunity for growth. It is your responsibility—and God's intention—for you to find and choose the opportunity side. This can be accomplished as you learn a more observing approach to life.

➤ Action Point 2

- Today, observe your own life rather than reacting to its potential problems. Write down what is different about the times you are able to observe instead of react.
- What specifically were you doing instead?
- What do others notice about you that is different when you were doing this?
- How can you do more of this?
- How, exactly, will you do it?
- Do this for one week, briefly writing down your observations.
- As you continue to do these things what other changes do you notice?

chapter nine

Do What Works — On Purpose

Even if you are on the right track, you'll get run over if you just sit there.

WILL ROGERS

Regardless of circumstances, each man lives in a world of his own making.

JOSEPHA MURRAY EMMS

I have a plaque hanging on the wall of my office that shows two men in a rowboat out at sea. Under the picture are the words, "Pray to God, but row toward shore." I've received a variety of responses from those who have viewed it. Some think it is amusing, others thought-provoking, still others are somewhat annoyed with it. Of course part of this is due to how we each develop our understanding of the world. Yet for me the plaque simply shows that the only proper response to prayer is to take action. In taking action we are now trusting God to guide our steps—sometimes into what may seem to be very treacherous territory. There may be occasions where we truly believe God is instructing us to stand still and watch what He is going to do, but on the whole, He is expecting us to move forward. As we do, He can and will guide us.

MOSES AND THE RED SEA

One of the most remarkable "pray-and-move" events was the Israelite Exodus out of Egypt and across the Red Sea. The

Israelite slaves were caught between the wilderness and the sea. It was God's intention for it to be so (Ex. 14:2–4), but the people still grumbled against Moses. "Weren't there enough graves for us in Egypt? Why did you make us leave?" they complained. But God had told Moses that the people would be delivered in a mighty, never-to-be-forgotten fashion. He said to them, "Don't be afraid. Stand where you are and watch the Lord rescue you." I'm sure this sounded appealing to the people. I know I would be ready to do nothing and let God rescue me. In fact, I would have gotten out my beach chair, thrown on some suntan lotion, and kicked back to wait. I think this is why God's next words to Moses must have really shaken him up, and the Israelites along with him. God said, "Why are you crying out to Me? Tell the people to get moving!"

"What? I thought we were going to watch *You* do it, Lord? Get moving where? The Egyptians and the wilderness are behind us, the sea is in front of us. I don't think so, Lord." And they would have stayed. *Stuck!* If they had not begun moving forward the sure result would have been a return to slavery. Of course we all know today that God parted the sea. But they did not know this was going to happen. Move forward into the unknown, or as the Living Bible puts it, "Quit praying and get the people moving! Forward march!" As they began to move, God parted the sea. And let me add, walking through that sea must have taken every ounce of courage they had. Walls of water on each side. Total trust in a "Hand" that was unseen. Yet, forward they went.

> We get so stuck, we cannot see a way to move forward. Even if we hear God saying, "Forward march!" we seem frozen in place.

Going forward is probably the surest sign of faith. As James said, "I will show you my faith by what I do" (James 2:18). But that is just the issue, is it not? We get so stuck, we cannot see a way to move forward. Even if we hear God saying, "Forward march!" we seem frozen in place. The marriage is still stuck. The situation with the teenage son or daughter still seems out of control. The company is downsizing just as the children have reached college age. So much bitterness has grown up in that relationship that it cannot be restored. We do not know what to think.

JOEL AND THE DUCKS

I am reminded of my nephew Joel. Now a grown man with a family of his own, there was an early occasion when he was stuck, not knowing what to do. He was only three years old, with the face of innocence—although his mom and dad would know better about that. My wife and I took him and his two older brothers to a pond to the feed the ducks. We were newly married, and of course we were sure we could handle anything three small, innocent children could send our way. So we gave each child his own full bag of bread, assured in our ignorance that the children would know what to do. For the most part they did . . . except for Joel.

Things were moving along smoothly until we noticed a whole mass of ducks converging on a single spot. There was such a commotion, everyone was running over to see what was happening. And there, nearly invisible, lost in the middle of the excitement, we could barely make out a small child—Joel. He had decided to dump the whole bag out on the ground, right at his feet. I'm sure he was quite surprised at the rush of feathers and bills that immediately came charging at him. Terrified, he stood perfectly still until I could retrieve him from the feeding frenzy. Afterward, we asked him why he did it. Looking up at us, eyes wide with wonder, he replied, "I . . . I just didn't think."

Today I laugh at the memory of my nephew's words. Yet, how many times have I done the same thing? I act in an uncaring way, or I become angry when I fail to get my way. Sometimes I become so focused on my problems that I freeze up, not knowing what to do next. When this happens, I can say along with little Joel, "I . . . I just didn't think." Perhaps you have had such moments yourself. You are frozen into inaction. Or, perhaps you act, but without thinking. When we do act, our actions flow out of perceptions that all too often fail to take into account God's intention. Unfortunately we then become locked in our perceptions. From what we think we see flows what we begin to believe—both about ourselves and others. If our perception is faulty, so also the meaning.

MEANING IS PERCEPTION

Let me clarify what I mean by this phrase, meaning is perception. I remember a time long ago when I was about eight years old. Sitting at the kitchen table with my family, we were eating some of my mom's delicious chicken soup. On this day, for whatever reason, I was seated next to my oldest brother who was then around fourteen. This was not our normal seating arrangement, however. As I glanced over at him I noticed that something was amiss. He had a little, dried "you-know-what" hanging from his nose. Worse than that, it was moving as he breathed, flapping in the wind, so to speak. I just *knew* it was going to break off and fly into my soup. The tension became unbearable—I had to move. But how? At age eight you do not just get up and ask someone to trade places with you for no reason.

It was unthinkable that I should tell him about his soon-to-take-flight dried excrescence. So what did I do? I told my mom I just *had* to move—no explanation given. After a brief exchange of words, which primarily focused on why I did not love my brother, I was moved. From my mother's perspective her youngest son did not love her eldest, and this brought to her a feeling of momentary sadness. That is, her perception created her meaning and from that meaning flowed her emotion. Yet, the perception was faulty. I just didn't want to get a flying "you-know-what" in my soup! My perception was on his nose, and the meaning was clear: run for the hills! I actually felt quite relieved once I moved.

Each day we create meaning for ourselves by our perceptions.

In this, and a thousand other ways each day we create meaning for ourselves by our perceptions. Of course, we will find ourselves truly restricted by our limited perceptions when our behaviors, which are our responses to what we believe to be true, are viewed as somehow predetermined. That is, we actually come to believe that how we behave is our *only* course of action.

Therefore, we begin to view our actions as being *caused* by our interactions with the world around us.

LATE AT THE GATE

There is a story I have often told that may or may not be exactly what it seems. Indeed, it sometimes changes even in the telling. It starts something like this. Some years ago, while still serving as a navy chaplain, I had trouble with my car. The ship was in port, and I was stranded on the pier while my car was being repaired. It was cold, midwinter, and my wife and I agreed that she would keep the good car and pick me up on the pier at 6:00. Well, 6:00 came and went, then 6:15 and 6:30. At 6:50 I called home from a phone booth and listened to my own voice on the answering machine. Most of my shipmates who could have given me a ride home were gone. When they offered I declined, since I *knew* my wife was coming to get me. Pacing back and forth to stay warm I finally saw car lights in the distance. It was my wife. As she pulled up I began to angrily wave her over, telling her to move aside from behind the steering wheel.

"Just move over, I'll drive." As I pushed my way into the car my wife began to say, "I'm sorry—" but I cut her off with a furious stare, huffing and puffing. "Just don't say a thing . . . okay!?" "But Charles, let me tell you—" "That's it," I said, cutting her off again. "I asked you to just not say anything," I growled out, warming up to my righteous indignation. "All I asked you to do is be here at 6:00. You don't have anything else to do all day but be here." (That went over real well!) "Just be quiet now and let me drive home in peace!" Sullenly, my wife responded, "Nathan is in the backseat [our then seven-year-old son]. We need to stop on the way home and get him a milk shake since he was such a good boy while getting stitches." Yes, there he was, looking at me with eyes wide open, watching his dad make a fool of himself. He had fallen and cut his arm, and that was why my wife had been late. She called the ship but they simply told her I had left.

Well, as I said, this story often changes in the telling. Let me back up a moment and suggest a different scenario. Perhaps something quite different took place. Six o'clock came and went, then 6:15 and 6:30. At 6:50 I called home from a phone booth and listened to my own voice on the answering machine. Most of my shipmates who could have given me a ride home were gone. Those who offered I had told no thanks, since I knew my wife was coming to get me. Pacing back and forth to stay warm I finally saw car lights in the distance. As my wife pulled up I walked over to the car window and said, "I was getting really worried. What happened?" Warmly, my wife responded, "Nathan is in the backseat. We need to stop on the way home and get him a milk shake since he was such a good boy while getting stitches." Yes, there he was, looking at me with eyes wide open, seeing his dad's love and concern.

Hold on now. Maybe the story unfolded in still a different way. Let me back up again and suggest another scenario. Six o'clock came and went. I huddled up to stay warm, taking out my Bible to read under the streetlight. Most of my shipmates who could have given me a ride home were gone. Those who offered I had told no thanks, since I knew my wife was coming to get me. Nearly an hour later I saw car lights in the distance. As my wife pulled up I walked over to the window as she was rolling it down. She quickly said, "I'm sorry I'm so late. Nathan is in the backseat. We need to stop on the way home and get him a milk shake since he was such a good boy while getting stitches." My only response was to say, "I didn't even know you were late; I was so busy reading my Bible. I'm glad Nathan is okay. What happened?"

Well, perhaps I am not quite *that* spiritual. Actually, the story is simply a way of illustrating one very important point. If the "event" of my wife picking me up late had *caused* my anger, then anger would have been my only possible response. As you can see from these scenarios, there were three possible responses: being angry, being worried, and being unaffected. There were probably numerous other possible reactions, each one bringing a different ending to the story. The only real difference in these story lines was *my* reaction—and my reaction was a direct result of my thoughts. Now consider this: My thoughts were a direct result of my *perception*. All of life is like this. Our thoughts act somewhat like a snowplow, preparing the way for good or evil responses. Being unaware of this just makes us easier to manipulate. And of course that is the Devil's stock-in-trade.

Recently, I advised a fellow who came to me for counsel to keep a silver dollar in his pocket. One side of the coin was to represent his difficult situation, which he could not control. The other side was to represent his response to that situation, which he could control. Like this man, we all too often relinquish the only part we actually have control over—our response—to try to change the part we often have little control over . . . the situation. Once we see this, we can focus more on our response. This, in turn, forces us to critique our perceptions— with God's intention being the benchmark. When we do this we can hear His voice saying, "Forward march!" and off we go— marveling as the sea parts before us. As we take one deliberate step forward, we will watch as the sea rolls back. And so we continue, one step at a time. Sometimes this can happen in the most unusual ways.

> **Our thoughts act somewhat like a snowplow, preparing the way for good or evil responses.**

THE DANCING MOM

A fellow counselor told me about a mother who came to him, along with her thirteen-year-old daughter. She was a single mom, and her relationship with her daughter had been suffering recently. She was now at a point where she did not know what to do. When they fought, it usually ended up in a physical altercation. During the course of the counseling interview she was asked if what she was doing was working. She said it was not, but in desperation she wondered what else she could do. The counselor suggested that she was "dancing the dance" with her daughter, caught up in doing the same thing over and over, even though it was not working. He suggested doing something different and doing it deliberately. In keeping with this advice, Mom came upon the idea of dancing whenever she was getting ready to yell. (It seems she took the "dancing the dance" idea more literally than the counselor intended!)

The following week the daughter came into his office first. He asked her if anything had improved, and she answered that it had. She stated that the fighting had stopped, but Mom had gone nuts. She explained that one evening in the car an argument had started, and right before it got out of hand her mom had pulled over. The daughter thought for sure that she was going to get hit. Instead, her mom got out of the car, walked over to a phone booth, went in, and started to dance! As it turned out, this so surprised her daughter that it interrupted the pattern that was leading to the terrible fights. Mom was no longer "dancing the fight dance" with her daughter—she was actually dancing! Therefore, her daughter had no one to fight with. I believe, even though the method was unusual, it gave room for God's Spirit to intervene and opened the door for more constructive solutions in counseling. Her daughter thought Mom had "gone crazy," but she was smiling when she said it.

Mom had made a decision to move from a reactive approach to a deliberate one. Have you ever had a doctor test your reactions with a little triangular rubber hammer? Your leg probably jumped all by itself. This is okay for legs or emergency situations, but bad for interactions in difficult circumstances, especially with difficult people. You see, reactions take place without our conscious thought. Remember that just because the brain is functioning does not mean that the mind is fully

> An unusual method may give room for God's Spirit to intervene and open the door for more constructive solutions.

alert and effective. For the mind to be fully effective it must originate deliberate actions and behaviors. But how can we become more deliberate? Can we really control our thoughts in this way? The answer is yes, but it takes practice.

Every time you do, it will get a little easier. Remember that you are entering into agreement with God's intention for how our brain is meant to work. You are developing spiritually mature habits. Pathways are being created that will help you see what you will do next. Yet, to do so you need to take captive every thought to make it obedient to Christ (2 Cor. 10:5)—you are growing into the mind of Christ. Develop the habit of slowing down your reactive impulse, and learn a more deliberate and purposeful approach to life and decision making.

CAPTURING REBEL THOUGHTS

One way to take every thought captive is to utilize an approach to stress and thought management that is biblically based. It will assist you in capturing your thoughts that daily seek to rebel against obedience to Christ. This approach can be summed up with four words: *Pause, Praise, Ponder,* and *Plan.* These are presented here to complement, not take the place of, the essential spiritual habits of discipleship and service. Let us take a moment to look at each step in turn.

Step One: Pause

"Life is what happens to us while we are busy making other plans" (Thomas la Mance). The apostle Paul wrote, "Examine yourselves to see whether you are in the faith; test yourselves" (2 Cor. 13:5). Often, in the midst of a stressful environment we get so caught up in the activities and plans of the day that we fail to examine ourselves, to test our perceptions. Are we walking in agreement with the Holy Spirit? What do our thoughts reveal? We will not discover an answer till we learn to slow down and think—to "pause." This seems simple, but it is actually profound. For example, why do we often fail to pray as we should? It is frequently because we simply do not stop to do so. In this case, pausing is the first step toward more deliberate behavior—including prayer.

For example, imagine that while you are driving, the red engine light comes on. What would you do? Hopefully you would stop at the nearest service station. The red light serves as a prompter to remind you what to do if the engine is having trouble. What kind of "red lights" did God give the human body? Again, Paul tells us the answer. To the ancient church of Colosse he wrote, "Let the peace of Christ rule in your hearts . . ." (Col. 3:15). This is not a "spiritual" truth for Sunday mornings, but a practical tool God has given to help you know what to do so that you can mature as His child. The "peace of Christ" is to rule and act like an umpire within all our relationships.

This is not simply an emotion of personal peace, but rather a signal from God that will help to maintain a healthy, loving environment. Paul is referring to unity and peace within relationships. He goes on to write, ". . . since as members of one body you were called to peace. And be thankful.* Unlike happiness, which is based solely on our exceedingly limited view of a situation, peace is a gift of God's grace given so we can create an environment where others feel safe and loved by us. Remember, the peace of Christ is an emotion of God, flowing straight from His thoughts. To have God's emotions you need to maintain God's thoughts.

But, do you listen to what your emotions are telling you? That is, what are you noticing about your own response to potentially stressful situations? If you are not at peace, there is a flashing red warning light on the dashboard of your soul. We ignore it only at our greatest peril. Much more than our car engine is at stake. Rather, the health of our very mind and our relationships are on the line. Remember the oxygen mask in the airplane? If your mind is not healthy, how can you give to your family, or even the stranger along the way that God wants you to minister to, what you do not have yourself? All we have to offer is peace. Theology just will not do. Money will help for a season. But peace is the true gift of love.

The peace of Christ is to rule and act like an umpire within all our relationships.

About His disciples' ministry Jesus said, "If the home is deserving, let your peace rest on it; if it is not, let your peace return to you" (Matt. 10:13). He also said, "If a son of peace is there, your peace will rest on it; if not, it will return to you" (Luke 10:6 NKJV). Interestingly, Jesus is teaching that it is through this "peace" that Christians are to recognize one another. Although an encounter with Jesus can result in hostility from those who harden their hearts (Matt. 10:34), this is always a response by others to God—and to God's children. It will not proceed *from* us when God is made to rule in our hearts and minds, for He brings peace. It is the true gift from Jesus to those who trust Him daily: "Peace

I leave with you; my peace I give you. I do not give to you as the world gives. Do not let your hearts be troubled and do not be afraid" (John 14:27). "Peace be with you" were the first words the disciples heard from Jesus after His resurrection (see Luke 24:36).

Because peace is such a great gift, our lack of peace should serve as a prompter to remind us to *do* something. Pull off the road! You could develop a simple prompter to help form a habit of pausing on a regular basis—even when you feel fine. Learn to do this when life is calm, so it will be second nature to do so when the storms roll in. A simple prompter can be made by purchasing small, blue stick-on dots. Place these on

> **Our lack of peace should serve as a prompter to remind us to do something.**

your watchband, phones, mirrors, and dashboard of your car to remind you to pause. Whenever you look at one, pause. (If you are crossing a street at the time, wait till you are on the other side!)

Whether you notice an unpleasant emotion other than peace, or you use a prompter such as the blue dots, you must find a way to bring yourself to pause on a regular basis; I recommend at least once every hour. But what do we do when we pause? We praise!

Step Two: Praise

During the course of the day it is easy to build up a level of stress that seems to never quite leave us once it appears. Your entire body is affected. You can get fatigued, irritable, and discouraged. Sometimes this can also lead to an increased state of anxiety or fearfulness. This should come as no surprise since stress is a physical reaction in your body. It is actually not an influence from outside of you, but a reaction *in* your body.

Consider for a moment what would happen if you were alone in your home at night and you awoke from a deep sleep at two in the morning. You decide to go to your kitchen and get something to drink. While pouring a glass of milk, you hear someone moving in the dark behind you. You freeze! What is happening in your body? Your heart is racing, your mouth is dry, and a feeling of cold sweat quickly covers your skin. You may almost feel faint. Your glass falls from your hand, crashing to the floor—your brain forgetting that your hand was holding it. Then, you discover that it was simply the cat moving. You take a deep breath and perhaps laugh at your reaction. Possibly you're angry at the cat. Either way, it takes five to ten minutes for your body to return to normal. Afterward, you have a splitting headache or stiff shoulders. What happened? Your brain just sent a massive dose of adrenaline, a hormone or neurotransmitter, into your body. Even after the threat is gone, it takes time for the adrenaline, also called norepinephrine, to be used up and get out of your system.

Effects of the brain's overproduction of norepinephrine can be recognized as a generalized panic or anxiety, headaches, general gastric distress, feelings of nausea, acid stomach and heartburn, diarrhea, some forms of colitis, indigestion, constipation, churning, neck aches and shoulder pain, stiff neck, teeth grinding, jaw joint pain, generalized pain in arms and legs, respiratory problems, some asthma, hyperventilation syndrome, shortness of breath, cold extremities, increased sweating, skin eruptions, general feelings of trembling, fear of impending doom, inability to sit long, squirming and fidgeting, foot tapping, pacing, feelings of fatigue, lack of energy, heightened irritability and anger, racing thoughts, daydreaming, indecisiveness, and sleep disruption. As if the previous list was not enough, the majority of heart disease is a direct result of this process.

Here is how the heart is weakened. Stressful *thoughts* originate in the cerebral cortex, the part of the brain that receives and sends messages and processes information. The cerebral cortex signals the adrenal glands to release norepinephrine, which speeds up your heart rate and breathing and makes your hands sweat. The blood courses through your body at increased pressure, eroding tiny cells on the lining of the coronary artery. Tiny clotting platelets then clump together on the damaged artery and release chemicals that stimulate muscle cells, which in turn swell and absorb *cholesterol*. Meanwhile, the norepinephrine stimulates fat cells, which empty into the bloodstream. If the fat is not burned, your liver converts it into more cholesterol, which collects in the artery. Over time, the cholesterol forms *plaque*, which may eventually block the artery and cause a heart attack.

Certainly a great deal is at stake when we fail to examine ourselves and to let the peace of Christ rule in our thoughts. Norepinephrine cuts off creative thinking and moves the body and mind into a reactive mode. This reaction has been called a "fight or flight" reflex. God installed this neurotransmitter to give us the extra energy we need to respond to an emergency. Unfortunately, in most of us, troublesome relationships and difficult situations also trigger this hormone.

Actively giving praise is commanded over 340 times in the Word of God.

Of course God created us knowing the potential dangers of norepinephrine, so He also created a safeguard: PRAISE! In Psalm 22:26 David sings, "They who seek the LORD will praise him—may your hearts live forever!" I believe praise will give us a more healthy heart, both emotionally and physically. In another place David sings, "Why are you downcast, O my soul? Why so disturbed within me? Put your hope in God, for I will yet praise him, my Savior and my God" (Ps. 42:5). Indeed, actively giving praise is commanded over 340 times in the Word of God.

So how do we praise? Well, for me it is virtually impossible to effectively praise God until I pause. Once I pause, I try to deliberately slow my heart rate down. In doing this I am sending a physical signal to my brain to stop producing norepinephrine. I begin by slowing my breathing down. Try breathing in slowly for a count of five, holding for a moment, then exhaling slowly, blowing out through your lips for another slow count of five. Wait a moment, and then do it again. This time as you breathe in slowly, imagine you are breathing in God's Spirit through the top of your head—clearing out your mind, quieting your thoughts. Then slowly exhale, blowing out all your frustration and discouragement. In fact, exhale whatever is bothering you. As you do, tell your mind and body to relax, and begin to softly give thanks to God for anything and everything. Offer true praise. Express your love and appreciation. Thank God for what is happening in your life, and for the knowledge of God's gentle intention that is unfolding. "Be joyful always; pray continually; give thanks in all circumstances, for this is God's will for you in Christ Jesus" (1 Thess. 5:16–18). Do this quieting exercise, breathing slowly, a few more times.

Also, try doing this for longer periods, perhaps in the evening. After you breathe in, hold your breath for five seconds and stretch all your muscles—just like a cat. Stretch from your feet to your face, and then gently blow out your frustrations, anger, or doubts. As you do, relax all your muscles, including your face and jaw. Do this again, breathing in God's Spirit and love, stretching, and blowing out your worry or fears. Then do the same exercise, but replace stretching with tensing your muscles.

When a muscle is either stretched or tensed, it will return to a state of deeper relaxation. This is important, because norepinephrine pumps blood into your muscles, causing all-too-familiar body aches. This exercise will quiet your spirit and relax your body. Also, when you are praising and rejoicing with your mind, your body will release cells into your immune system that will actually increase the health of your brain. Do this whenever you either look at your prompter, or when your emotions reveal to you that you have parted company with the peace of Christ. If you include a brief time of prayer as you praise you will begin to discover more ways to fulfill Paul's injunction to pray continually.

> When you are praising and rejoicing with your mind, your body will release cells into your immune system that will actually increase the health of your brain.

Step Three: Ponder

"Life consists of what a man is thinking of all day" (Ralph Waldo Emerson).

Having learned how to deliberately slow down, to pause and quiet our hearts and thoughts with praise, now we are ready to truly examine ourselves. At this point we can critique our thoughts, taking captive each one to make it obedient to Christ. To do so we need a plumb line. Builders use these to help them ensure that a wall is straight. The prophet Amos said that God would set a plumb line to reveal the crookedness of His people Israel. So also, we need a mental plumb line to reveal our "crooked" thinking. Such thinking is like looking through a pair of glasses that are the wrong prescription. Everything is distorted. So also crooked or "distorted" thinking affects all else that we see and feel, as well as our behaviors.

When I examine my thoughts, I ask myself if I am using the following thought patterns in any way: blaming, self-reproach, catastrophizing, overgeneralizing, and all-or-nothing thinking. When we indulge in any of them we bring about the release of norepinephrine and increase all the risks associated with the emotions, behaviors, and physical symptoms of distress that result from such a continual release. Let us examine each one individually.

The first pattern of thinking, blaming, is a truly destructive force in our thought life. As I have stated previously, blaming started with Adam in the Garden. "The man said, 'The woman you put here with me—she gave me some fruit from the tree, and I ate it'" (Gen. 3:12). Not only is it not my fault, it's Your fault, God! Blaming is the opposite of accepting responsibility for our emotions and actions. It occurs when a person seeks to point at someone else (or something else) when an unpleasant situation occurs. Common statements include, "It's your fault"; "You should have known better"; or "This is all his fault." When we are in a blaming position, we cannot come into agreement with God, nor can we walk with Him. Our thoughts betray our loss of peace.

The second pattern of thinking, self-reproach, is blaming turned inward. When using self-reproach statements, an individual thinks about how he or she has not lived up to some standard—which is usually very vaguely defined. Peter was in anguish for not living up to his own standards, never realizing that it was the Lord's intention for him to learn and grow into a leader through his mistakes. Instead of thinking about what he wanted, he thought only about how he *should* be. So with this thought pattern. Common self-reproach statements usually include words like "should" and "must." For example, "I should never have let that happen"; "I must get there on time"; "I must get this done today"; and "If I make a mistake, it means I'm stupid." Equally destructive—the peace of Christ is lost and brain pathways are formed that, if not changed, will lead to some very unpleasant and unproductive personality traits.

The third pattern of thinking, catastrophizing, is the old-fashioned "making a mountain out of a molehill." In this case, the person thinks the worst. Rather than thinking that the situation or relationship is disagreeable, it is viewed as a tragedy. The ten spies came back to Moses and said, "The land we explored devours those living in it. All the people we saw there are of great size. . . . We seemed like grasshoppers in our own eyes, and we looked the same to them" (Num. 13:32–33). Don't we do the same today? Common phrases heard when catastrophizing include "This is horrible"; or "I can't believe it, this is awful"; or "This is the worst thing I could imagine; my life is ruined."

> **When an individual's focus is so firmly fixed on a problem, seeing potential solutions becomes increasingly difficult.**

At this point, the individual's focus is so firmly fixed on the problem that seeing potential solutions becomes increasingly difficult. In the case of Israel, they became stuck for forty years.

The fourth pattern of thinking, overgeneralizing, forces the person's thoughts and feelings away from the specific situation by generalizing on other things. Common words include "always," "never," and "forever." The King of Israel said that the prophet Micaiah *always* prophesied bad things about him. This was not true. The prophet simply spoke what God told him to say, nothing more and nothing less (1 Kings 22:8). When we do this today it usually sounds something like, "This *always* happens to me" and "Things will *never* change." Overgeneralized thoughts serve as a self-fulfilling prophecy of the future and lead to a feeling of hopelessness.

The fifth pattern of thinking, all-or-nothing, occurs when the individual emphasizes the extremes of situations while ignoring the "middle ground." The rich young ruler walked away from Jesus when Jesus told him to give away his money to the poor. It never crossed his mind that Jesus was the only source of true wealth. Since he did not get what he wanted, he immediately left, angry and sad. Of course, this happens all too often today as well. Events are viewed as all bad or all good. So also, people are viewed as having all positive or all negative qualities. For example, a special evening may be planned and one wrong look spoils *everything*. Or, a person wakes up late for work and decides not to go in at all, now lying to support his position. In either case, *all-or-nothing* thinking locks the person into extreme positions. When the world or a relationship does not conform to expectations, the reaction is excessive, resulting in further destructiveness to the situation.

On occasion I have known persons to put all five criteria into one statement: "I can't believe this! What a lousy driver! Why do I always get stuck behind people like this? This always happens to me. Now I'm going to be late. I might as well not go at all!" This person is going to have a massive headache and probably spread a few around for others.

Step Four: Plan

Have you ever heard the joke about the man who went to the doctor with an arm that hurt when he lifted it a certain way. When he was able to see the doctor he held up his arm in the position that hurt and said, "Doc, it hurts when I do this." The doctor's reply was, "Don't do that!" So also with these criteria. First pause, then praise—quieting your spirit in the Lord. Then evaluate your thoughts. If you find yourself indulging in any of those negative thought patterns, "Don't do that!"

When you are observing, you are not reacting. This creates a positive self-perpetuating cycle.

Instead, plan to succeed. Ask yourself, "What will I be doing *instead* of blaming, self-reproach, catastrophizing, overgeneralizing, and using all-or-nothing thinking?" Then, equally important, "What will it look like when I do this?"

Using these four words—pause, praise, ponder, plan—will help you develop true internal strength and create new patterns of thinking, out of which will flow real solutions to the problems you face.

Key Points and Action Steps for Personal Application

KEY POINT 1

You will find yourself severely restricted by limited perceptions when you believe that your behavior, which is your response to what you believe to be true, is predetermined. In a thousand ways each day you are creating meaning for yourself—through your perceptions. In so doing you may come to believe that how you are presently behaving is your *only* course of action. In this way you begin to view your actions as being *caused* by your interactions with persons and situations.

➤ **Action Step 1**

- Your reactions are a direct result of your thoughts. Your thoughts are a direct result of your perceptions. Thus, your thoughts prepare the way for good or evil responses. This week, develop a habit of slowing down your reactive impulse. Strongly question any perceptions that lead you into thoughts that result in reactions that God would be displeased with. Keep a record of your observations. Act in a more deliberate and purposeful way this week, writing down what happens that is different every time you have been successful. Utilize observational skills you have previously been developing.

KEY POINT 2

True strength is always internal. As Solomon wrote, "Like a city whose walls are broken down is a man who lacks self-control" (Prov. 25:28). When you are without control of your own thoughts you may become a target when the Adversary attacks through your own thought life. To have God's emotions you need to maintain God's thoughts. The "peace of Christ" is to rule and act like an umpire within all your relationships.

> **Action Step 2**

- Utilize the "pause, praise, ponder, and plan" procedure to manage your thought life and develop more deliberate actions. A summary of the process follows.

1. PAUSE: When you are experiencing intense or heavy emotions, imagine the "red-light prompter." The red light, as on a car dashboard, reminds you to slow down and deliberately pull off the road. You can also use the "blue-dot prompter" to remind yourself to pause every hour or so throughout the day.

2. PRAISE: Begin a quieting exercise as you slow your breathing down. Inhale slowly for a count of five, hold for a moment, and then exhale slowly, blowing out through your lips for another slow count of five. Wait a moment and then do it again. This time as you slowly breathe in, imagine you are breathing in God's Spirit through the top of your head—clearing out your mind, quieting your thoughts. Then slowly exhale, blowing out all your frustration, discouragement, or whatever may be bothering you. As you do, tell your mind and body to relax and begin to softly give thanks to God. Again, do this at least every hour—whenever you look at your prompter, or notice intense or heavy emotions.

   Do this exercise for ten to fifteen minutes once a day as well—adding stretching and tensing. After you inhale, hold your breath for five seconds and gently stretch all your muscles—like a cat. Stretch from your feet to your face, then slowly exhale your frustrations, anger, or doubts. As you do, relax all your muscles, including your face and jaw. Do this again, breathing in God's Spirit and love, stretching, and blowing out your worry or fears. Repeat this exercise, but replace stretching with tensing all your muscles. Now rest quietly for a moment. Do a PMC (present moment connector), noting what things you hear or feel. Repeating this longer exercise once a day will train your body to recognize this more relaxed state when you pause and praise each hour during the day. Your short exercise, when you use the prompter throughout the day, will trigger your body's experience of relaxation and well-being that you have developed during the longer exercise.

3. PONDER: Having paused and quieted your heart and thoughts with praise, now begin to critique your thoughts, checking yourself against the list of thought patterns. In your thoughts or words are you blaming anyone or anything for an unpleasant situation? Common statements include, "It's your fault"; "You should have known better"; or "This is all his fault." Are you allowing self-reproach to enter into your thoughts? Common self-reproach statements include words like "should" and "must." For example, "I should never have let that happen"; "I must get there on time"; "I must get this done today"; or "If I make a mistake, it means I'm stupid." Have you been permitting yourself to catastrophize? Common phrases when catastrophizing include "This is horrible"; "I can't believe it, this is awful"; or "This is the worst thing I could imagine; my life is ruined." Are you overgeneralizing? When you are, you think thoughts like, "This *always* happens to me"; "He *always* does that"; "Things will *never* change"; or "This will go on *forever*." Are you allowing all-or-nothing images to intrude into your thoughts and conversations? Some all-or-nothing thoughts or statements are, "The whole evening is now ruined"; or "If I can't win I won't play." All-or-nothing thinking locks you into extreme positions with excessive reactions—giving you, and others, no way out. With each of the thought patterns, your thoughts serve as self-fulfilling prophecies of the future and result in increased feelings of anger and hopelessness—often resulting in conversational and relational dead ends.

4. PLAN: Remember, your mind requires deliberate actions and behaviors. Pausing, praising, and pondering create

the opportunity to now think, and therefore act, in a planned and purposeful way. Ask yourself what you will be thinking *instead* of blaming, self-reproach, catastrophizing, overgeneralizing, or using all-or-nothing thought patterns. Also, think through the implications. How will you then act when you think this? What will you be doing differently? Deliberately visualize the opposite of how you were thinking and behaving, and *do* a little bit of that. Remember to notice what happens in you and around you in your emotions and interactions with others. Write down in your notebook what occurs when you are observing and not reacting to the activities and pressures of each day.

chapter ten

Problems Are Problems

Love does not consist in gazing at each other, but in looking together in the same direction.

ANTOINE DE SAINT-EXUPERY

The closest to perfection a person ever comes is when he is filling out a job application form.

ANONYMOUS

We live in a society that has become increasingly litigious, always looking for someone or something to blame for our difficulties. It is like Barney's song, maddeningly reversed, and put on a continuous loop. You know the tune, "I blame you, you blame me, we're an angry fam-i-ly . . ." Right or wrong, we co-exist with imperfect people. I recall when my brother was frustrated with an experience he had with some people at a church he was attending. I suggested that if he ever found a perfect church he should be sure not to attend there. Taking the bait, he asked me why. Well, the answer was obvious. As soon as he walked in the front door, the church would no longer be perfect! Of course the same would be true if I walked in—just ask my wife! I guess a perfect church could not have any people in it at all!

This is a grim, yet somehow liberating, truth. We do live in an imperfect world. Plenty of things are unfair. But that is why most of the problems we encounter are actually a combination of observable events. For example, as a teenager I attended a driver's education class. They showed quite cleverly how most accidents occurred. In one movie reel the story focused on three different cars. The driver of each was doing the best he or she could, yet each made an error at the same time that resulted in a fatal accident. As the cars were approaching one another, the mother in one is seen briefly looking over her shoulder at her baby snugly secured in a car seat. The businessman in another is quickly glancing at his car radio to put on his favorite station. The husband in the third car is in the midst of an argument with his wife. Taking his eyes off the road he strays to the right just a little. The mother, glancing up, overreacts—swerving her car out of the lane. The businessman will never find that radio station as he is killed instantly—along with the mother and the baby . . . and a husband who will never get the chance to say he is sorry to his wife.

Each event on its own was not out of the ordinary. They represent actions, or behaviors, that most of us have made while driving. It was the combination of events, or the *interaction,* that made them deadly. Much of life is like this. It is the timing and style of the interaction that results in the fight or argument. We may choose to blame the other person or persons, but if we could stand apart from our lives and see these moments with a "bird's-eye" view, we would discover a rich interplay of events. The actions, reactions, and counteractions to so many of our "problems" would be clearly visible. Remember that God's intention includes all of these possibilities, weaving them into our lives to accomplish His purposes. But, as we have previously seen, our perceptions are laughably incomplete. Our "data" is insufficient. For this reason the Enemy can deceptively manipulate our short-sightedness—turning us against one another—and in our anger, against God. So what is really happening here?

BLAME IT ON STAR TREK

The Millers were "seekers" but not yet Christians and had become consumed with finger-pointing. In fact, at our first session the wife unrolled a sheet of paper with over fifty complaints against her husband. She had been keeping a record! The list actually opened like a scroll. I felt like I had inadvertently found myself at the Great White Throne of Judgment (Rev. 20:11)! But this was just the beginning. Her husband had yet to fire a shot. He was certainly not a shrinking violet. As his salvos crossed her bow, the temperature in my office began to rise as accusation piled upon accusation. I do not allow heated exchanges in marital counseling, seeking instead to discover God's solutions rather than rehashing and focusing on the couple's problems. But this was one of a small number of couples I have counseled that could take control of the session with their bickering and blaming, and my jaw would just hang open.

This pattern was repeated in one form or another over the course of four or five sessions. I always knew when I had an appointment with the Millers—I would begin to sweat! Apart, they were fine. Together was another story. I was baffled. Is not God active in their lives . . . somewhere? Seeing them was a test to my faith that they were not even aware of. The Millers were a thirty-something couple. Like so many of their generation, they had grown up on television. So I took a shot at a different approach.

"Did either of you ever watch *Star Trek*? Not the new shows, but the old ones from the sixties with Kirk, Spock, and company?" Their response was a devoted yes, so I knew I was onto something. I remembered one particular show that might shed some light on their situation . . . if only they had seen it. "Do you remember when the crew of the Enterprise was trapped on a 'death ship' with the Klingons? They were filled with hate and violence—killing each other repeatedly, yet they could not die. It turned out that there was a merciless alien entity on the ship with them. It looked like a fiery, spinning vortex that was actually feeding off of their hate and violence." (You have to use words like "vortex" with Trekkies!) The Millers vigorously nodded and smiled at the memory of this "classic." "Yeah, we saw that one," they enthusiastically replied. "It was a red spinning thing that followed them around, and it grew larger and stronger with the crew's hate," Mr. Miller added.

This was the response I had hoped for, so I continued. "You know, I think something like that is happening with you two. It is as if there is a fiery, spinning, laughing, evil *thing* that is just having all kinds of fun at your expense! It is hanging there, feeding off your blame and accusations. Like a growing cancer, it is mocking you and thoroughly enjoying each and every complaint, insinuation, and slur. Indeed, it is encouraging you to increase your finger-pointing and criticism. It thrives on it!" The whole time I was describing this "alien entity" I was looking into the upper corner of the room, speaking in a sneering and mocking fashion. All of our eyes were focused on "IT," and you could almost see it, viciously, mockingly spinning up there.

Something happened! They looked at each other, back at the "entity," over at me, back at each other, back at the "alien" . . . and a look of understanding and awareness washed over their faces. It was clear that the jig was up for the "alien." It had been discovered. I gave the Millers one instruction at the end of our session. "Whenever you begin to blame, criticize, or point fingers at each other, I want you to look up to the corner of the room and see this thing laughing at you—enjoying your performance!" When they returned the following week they were a different couple. They looked like honeymooners. They sat together for the first time, and they were actually . . . "snuggling!"

The change has continued since that day. It turns out for the Millers that blame was the problem, not one another. They both had too much *pride* to allow this "thing" to get the best of them. The difference is that their pride, which had been constantly directed at one another, was now directed at a common foe! This made all the difference in the world.

Now, before you think that this was all based on my silly imagination, that there never was a malevolent "alien entity," let me remind you that the apostle Paul taught us that our struggle is not against flesh and blood. Rather, it is against the rulers, against the authorities, against the powers of this dark world, and against the spiritual forces of evil in the heavenly realms (Eph. 6:12). Satan is the adversary and the accuser. The "Entity" exists!

Stop focusing on a person as the problem. The problem is the problem.

Equally important is that God was already at work, as He always is. The clues of His activity and preparation can be found in some of the most unusual places—even in an old sixties sci-fi.

He had planted seeds that would eventually be used by His Spirit to rescue this couple from the deception of the Enemy. What has He placed into your life? Stop focusing on that person as the problem. The *problem* is the problem.

THE WILSONS' SON

Jerry and Darleen Wilson were becoming more and more concerned about their sixteen-year-old son, James. He seemed to be out of control these days. His grades had fallen, and he had become increasingly violent in his emotions and abusive in his behaviors. As the proverbial rebel without a cause, he was a one-man wrecking crew for this family. Many prayers were forthcoming, but it seemed that everything they tried to do simply made things worse. The patience of their three younger daughters had long since run out as well. When they brought James to me, it was with the clear conviction that *he* was the problem. And, to a certain extent, this was true.

I began to meet with James, and sometimes his mom or dad. The Wilsons' goal was to secure a change in James's behavior. After a number of visits, this change was not forthcoming. Rather, the tension was increasing, so I asked to see the whole family together. It did not take long to discover that this family was stuck in its perception of itself. James was the bad son whom no one could understand—and who could not understand himself either. His sister, Julie, one year younger, was the long-suffering child who was deeply hurt by her brother's bad behavior. Little sisters, Trina and Leslie (ages nine and eleven), were the professional observers—taking sides against big brother James when convenient to their cause. Dad was the frustrated, absentee father who was working harder and harder, but rarely seeing his children. And Mom was the suffering disciplinarian. She knew her cause was just, but could not get James or her family to change.

The first time they came to see me as a family, some of these entrenched "roles" that the Wilsons were stuck in began to be revealed. At its most basic biological level, what they were doing was not working because they had come to the limit of their neural pathways. What I mean is that they could not see any options because they had no personal or corporate experience to guide them. Now that they were stuck, they were doing what most of us do when we get stuck—blaming someone else for the problems. So, blame was rampant. Yet, they did have various resources that could be utilized if specifically harnessed. Their focus

When we get stuck, most of us blame someone for our problems.

needed to be moved from what was not working—what was stopping them from having a more satisfying family life—to a perspective that would enable them to see new possibilities and options.

As satisfying as it may have been to view James as the source of the family's problems, this approach left him with nowhere to go. His role had become well established over the years. Any child with backbone will act even worse if that behavior is expected of him! "If that is what everyone thinks, then that is what I will do!" is the teen's unspoken capitulation to the designated family role. Although this perception may have been earned through repeated bad behaviors, now this way of viewing him was becoming a self-fulfilling prophecy. Throughout this book I have presented some of the assumptions I bring to counseling—as well as to life. Let's take a look at how they applied to the Wilsons.

1. This family needs to tap into its collective imagination. Up to this point their imaginations were being used, perhaps manipulated by outside forces (Eph. 6:12), to lock them into their perceived roles. No way out there, unless a new perception replaces the old.
2. They truly are the experts on their lives, and they have the ability to become experts at life as they learn together how to come more intentionally into agreement with the Master.
3. At present, this family is stuck. Their difficulties are not necessarily the tip of a mythical iceberg, that is, symptoms of deeper dysfunctions. Rather, their problems represent the limits of the family's combined perceptions—of themselves and of each other.

4. Not only is change inevitable, but they can seize the opportunity to change in a way that leads toward new solutions rather than toward a continuation of their problem.

5. Although these problems may seem complex, the solutions need not be. "Keep it simple" is still the rule.

6. God has already touched their lives. I want to come into agreement with what God is already doing; God's intention is the priority, so I am looking for clues of His activity.

7. I assume that there is something that every member of this family is willing to do. They will each want to get involved if it actually makes a difference in their lives, that is, the family is happier.

8. When the family can begin to visualize their lives without the dominance of this problem, this new perception will see them doing something that is different. Exploring this difference is the difference that will make a difference.

9. When this family starts to engage in actions that actually work, they can begin to do more of the same on purpose—observing what is working and doing more deliberately.

10. It is the problem that is the problem—not any one individual.

All ten assumptions present new possibilities to explore—each one shedding light on this family in a new way. Let us now focus on the final assumption.

In the vast majority of cases, the primary problem is the way family members are interacting. For the Wilsons, it is essential that each one learn that no member of the family is the problem. Mom and Dad are not the problem, James is not the problem, and his sisters are not the problem. Rather, the way they are *interacting* is the problem. This assumption will help free all parties from viewing each other as the problem, and make them a team in dealing with a common problem—the interaction.

Change the interaction in a deliberate way, jointly agreed upon, and the family is on the way to a more satisfying family life.

Thus, James will no longer be viewed as the problem. Neither will any other member of the family view herself or himself, or any other family member, as the problem. Instead, the problem is the problem. Rather than discouraging this family, they need to be empowered, to create a potential for improvement. This approach is in keeping with God's declared intention. His Spirit has brought about a new creation in Christ. I want to help this family proceed forward into it.

WILLINGNESS AND FIRE WALLS

After listening to the Wilsons, I clearly understood that they were all pointing fingers in blame. Also, they would form impromptu alliances at any given time to support one member or another. The way this would work is that James would blame Julie for some perceived infraction—and Trina would jump in to support Julie. Dad would point his finger at James—and Mom would enter in to express her frustration with James as well. Leslie would express anger toward James—and Julie would join in to voice her agreement. James would now become angrier with Julie—and all the family would begin yelling at James. Round and round it goes, where it stops nobody knows. Most of the individual perceptions are flawed in one form or another, and as tempers rise, the ability to reason together slowly fades into the distance.

When I called a time-out, I had only one question I wanted to ask to break up this logjam. Before I asked it I began with the following words. "In just a moment I am going to ask you all one question. You will only have a second to decide on your answer. I will simply say, 'One, two, three,' and you will have to answer quickly. If your answer is yes, raise your hand right away. If no, do not raise your hand. Here is the question. Do you want to live in a happy family? One, two, three!".... All five hands shot up into the air! Just this quickly we had something that the whole family was in agreement on. They all wanted to live in a happy family—they simply did not know how to get there!

Earlier that year in Virginia Beach, where I live, there had been a fire that spread from one apartment to ultimately consume

five. A number of persons lost their lives and afterward it was
determined that the apartment complex had been built without
the required fire walls between the individual apartments. Therefore, the fire spread more quickly than it otherwise would have,
and lives were lost. I mentioned this story to the Wilsons and they
all remembered the event. I suggested that their family had also
built without fire walls. When a fire, or angry reaction, began in
one "apartment," that is, one family member, there was nothing
in place to stop the fire from spreading. Therefore, the fire was
free to sweep though the whole family in a matter of moments.

Thus, if James was angry regarding any particular issue, the
fire was not contained within his own perception of frustration.
Rather, it quickly spread to Dad, Julie, Trina, or any other family member because they would enter in by reacting to his anger.
Of course this would set up further reactions from other family
members, as well as another response from James, and the fire
would consume the family. I was curious as to whether the
Wilsons could offer a way to keep this fire from spreading. Was
there any way they had accomplished this in the past? What
would *their* fire walls look like? Mr. Wilson recalled times that
he chose to stay out of an argument between Julie and James, and
that the problem seemed to take care of itself. Other family members recalled times they did the same in other situations, with different family members.

James then suggested a way for his family to begin building
some fire walls between individual "apartments." He laughingly
offered a simple slogan: "Only you can prevent forest fires!" He
suggested that if anyone entered into another person's anger or
frustration, that any other family member could remind him or
her to keep the fire contained by stating this simple slogan. I
thought this was creative and worth trying, so I asked if the rest
of the family would be interested in doing this for one week. All
gave permission—which was the first thing the Wilsons had
agreed upon for some time.

Also, based on their observations regarding past times that
family arguments had not escalated, I suggested that each family
member have his or her disagreements with only one other family

member at a time—with no other member entering into the conversation. This, along with James's humorous slogan, was my only task offered to the family. We finished for the day. The following week all agreed that arguments and "fires" had decreased. When I asked how they had managed to do this, they all replied that their individual "fire walls" were in place.

Interestingly, all focus had been on James as the source of this family's problems. Yet, it was when the family viewed the problem as the problem that they finally began to make some progress. In this way the family imagination was tapped into. A new perception of the problem was introduced, which permitted the Wilson family to get unstuck. We turned away the thought of symptoms representing deeper dysfunctions, focusing instead on their family's perception of themselves.

We sought to keep it simple, getting on track toward a solution, and since I believed that their lives had already been touched by God, our goal was to come into agreement with what He had already placed into their imaginations. Every member of this family wanted to live in a happy home environment and was willing to do something different to achieve this goal—as long as blame was put out of the way. We discovered that they each did want to get involved if it actually made a difference in their lives.

At this point the Wilsons began to visualize their home without this "fire" spreading so quickly, and each could clearly see his or her part in the solution. At our next session, and the few times we met afterward, they were engaged in actions that were actually working, observing what was working, and doing more on purpose. It was clear that a shift in thinking had taken place, and they began to

> The Master never views one person as the problem, but seeks to encourage partnership through working together toward a common purpose.

recognize a growing expertise in this area of how to stop family arguments from escalating so quickly. This new ability opened possibilities for healthier relationships within the family. In this fledgling attempt they demonstrated the kinds of decisions necessary for mastering life—and I believe they were more in agreement with the Master of life.

What about James? Did his life suddenly and dramatically change due to this new family partnership? Yes and no. He will still need to grow up, and only time will tell whether he will more fully master his life. Yet, his environment is now more conducive to his ultimate success. *The* Master never views one person as the problem, but seeks to encourage partnership through working together toward a common purpose. If I may paraphrase the apostle Paul's words written to the church at Ephesus: "Our families are no longer to be tossed back and forth by the storms of life and thrown here and there by every lie of the enemy and flame of anger. Instead, speaking the truth in love, we will in all things grow up into the mind of Christ. God's sovereign intention will unfold as the whole family is joined and held together *by* each and every other family member, growing and building itself up in love, as each member of the family does his or her part" (see Eph. 4:14–16).

AQUARIUMS AND HEALTHY FISH

Solomon wrote, "Many are the plans in a man's heart, but it is the LORD's purpose that prevails" (Prov. 19:21). Do you believe this? I do. I believe the Lord's purpose will prevail in your family and in your life. Our responsibility is *not* to make this happen. If we could do that, we would not be in need of a Savior. Rather, our responsibility is to *remove the barriers* to God's purpose. We want to create a balanced environment where we and our families can become healthy. Health then opens the door to new possibilities to grow and be built up in love.

What is a balanced environment? Perhaps you have at one time or another had a fish aquarium. If so, you know how much effort is expended in creating an environment where your fish will thrive. Unfortunately, I am a goldfish killer. The last time my daughter had one, I found it six months later under the cushion of my couch. It was as hard as a rock and I mistook it for one of my son's fishing lures. My brother and his wife, on the other hand, have a beautiful aquarium. The tank is kept heated to just the right temperature, the water is carefully oxygenated, and the exact amount of food is lovingly portioned out each day. This balanced environment is painstakingly maintained. Of course only God can create a fish, give it life, and make it beautiful. The responsibility my brother and his wife have is to give it an environment where it can naturally thrive.

Yet like the two-sided coin, many of us spend more of our time trying to change the things we cannot change, and not enough time seeking to change the things we can. We cannot cause our children's or spouse's growth—indeed, we cannot even cause our own! What we can do is create an environment where God's growth will naturally unfold. This balanced environment needs to be carefully maintained. What is it? It is an environment where persons feel loved, accepted, and forgiven. It is what God so care-

> **Our responsibility is to remove the barriers to God's purpose.**

fully prepared for us through the cross—and we now receive and offer to our loved ones. Remove the barriers to such an environment—allow family members to feel loved, accepted, and forgiven—and God's purpose will reveal itself unforced. Try to force it, and your very trying will harden the family "roles," as well as your own, and keep everyone stuck in place.

This is why I strongly encourage parents to make a gradual shift from parenting to mentoring when children are around twelve years old. If we remain in a parenting role as our children move into adolescence, we leave our teenagers only one role for themselves. If you remain the parent, then he or she remains the child. Few teens are comfortable with this

> **An environment of love, acceptance, and forgiveness creates a place for God's plan for growth to naturally unfold.**

role, and many rebel against it. Mentoring in love leaves little to rebel against. Our goal for children is to train them to behave the way we want them to, and to not behave in ways we do not approve of. When they become teenagers we begin bringing them slowly into our adult world. They need to learn more about our struggles and failures as they grow through these years. We become essential sources of information, sometimes giving them a precious bit of our experience at just the right time so they will know what to do next in their own lives. I realize this may be hard to accept, but we become more like an older brother or sister than a mom or dad. Of course we are always Mom or Dad, but as Christians we *do* have the same Father as our children—which will ultimately make us siblings.

Thus, we gradually increase their freedoms. With increased freedom comes increased responsibility. Our children learn through trial and error, coming home with their bumps and bruises that life sends their way. They need to feel safe and comfortable coming to us, their parents, as their primary source of information. If we continue to "parent" for too long, they will go to their friends and associates for this essential information—and that is a truly scary thought. Unmade minds are much more frightening to me than unmade beds!

Of course, this is also true about our commitment to God. We all start with a parent-child relationship, but God's purpose is for us to have the "mind of Christ," not to remain a child in

If you remain the parent, then your teen remains the child.

Christ. As He gradually gives us increased freedoms, we also have increased responsibilities. For example, we are no longer to be simply part of the crowd on Sunday mornings in church. Rather, we begin to move into a more committed position of membership and mutual accountability to our church family. In time we enter into the ministry of the church, helping in one of a variety of ways available to a maturing Christian within a local congregation.

Yet, ultimately we are to embrace the church's mission, catching its vision, reaching back out to the community around us with the good news of God's love, acceptance, and tender forgiveness. We become a part of our Lord's ministry of reconciliation and restoration. In this fashion, the church truly becomes our family—as God says it is. Pastors will want to create a balanced environment where the family can become healthy. Church-family health then opens the door to new possibilities to grow and be built up in love. In this regard it would be good to keep in mind that if we have ever felt hurt by someone in the church, that person in the church is *not* the problem. Rather, the problem is the problem. It is the interaction, and God has already factored all this into your development—and it is the Lord's purpose that will prevail.

STARK NAKED

One of the things you may not know about me is that I used to be a rock star . . . at least in my own mind. Back in the late sixties and early seventies I traveled with a number of bands, and one I briefly played with was called "Stark Naked."—Don't ask! Little did I know that this unfortunate name would someday be the answer for a couple who would come to me for help. This young married couple had discovered that after three years of marriage they had begun to argue bitterly much too often; they were completely embroiled in anger and frustration. Little we tried was helpful for them since their anger would rise up to defeat the best of plans.

I decided to ask them the following question: "On a scale from one to ten, where ten is 'I will do anything to save my marriage,' and one is 'I have given up on this marriage,' where would you put yourselves at the moment?" They made it clear that they were both at a ten. They emphatically agreed that they would do *anything,* so I told them a story about a couple I had read about who had a similar problem with arguing.

This other couple had been directed to pause whenever a fight was starting and go together to their bathroom. There they could continue their argument—but only after they stripped down and the husband sat in the bathtub dressed only in his "birthday suit," and the wife sat on the toilet seat in her "altogether."

As we were laughing about the image this brought to mind, I suggested that since these two were willing to do *anything,* they might actually benefit from trying this as well. Their mouths opened, then shut, and they looked at each other and agreed to the idea.

At our next session they came in with a somewhat sheepish look, giggling nervously. I simply asked them if anything had improved, and they broke into laughter. They had begun to fight and the wife had reminded her husband that they had promised each other to pause, strip down, and head for the bathroom to continue their argument. Her husband reluctantly agreed, throwing his clothing in anger around the room. Yet, when they actually looked at each other sitting in the tub and on the toilet stark naked, they burst out laughing. They were simply unable to treat each other in a mean or cruel way.

> Blame of any sort cuts us off from our key resources—one another.

The experience had such an impact on them that they had no serious arguments all week. Since they now realized they had some more control over the problem, knowing that they were able to do this, we began to explore other options by which the same outcome could be achieved—although I wouldn't be at all surprised if this became their favorite alternative.

As we imagine and work for solutions to problems, we become free to work together with others in seeking these same solutions. Blame of any sort cuts us off from our key resources—one another.

A HARSH TASKMASTER

Unfortunately, our perceptions often get in the way of what God is clearly seeking to accomplish in our lives. Remember the story of the talents? The one who had received a single talent trusted his own perception of his master. This faulty perception then corrupted his thoughts and ultimately his actions. Listen to it once again: "Then the man who had received the one talent came. 'Master,' he said, 'I knew that you are a hard man, harvesting where you have not sown and gathering where you have not scattered seed. So I was afraid and went out and hid your talent in the ground. See, here is what belongs to you,'" (Matt. 25:24–25). He felt the master was a "hard man" who would be unfair in his dealings with his servants. His trust was diminished as a result of this perception—and he became ineffective.

> The reason we do not enjoy the true freedom of simply loving others is because of our faulty understanding of God.

I do not believe anyone can rebel against the true God. We rebel against a "straw man," a caricature of the Creator. Even though God is love, we construct in our own minds a god in our own image, that is, a god who fits our vastly limited understanding of the universe. Many people can only rebel against this lie. There is nothing to fear from Perfect Love. Thus the apostle John wrote, "And so we know and rely on the love God has for us. God is love. Whoever lives in love lives in God, and God in him" (1 John 4:16); and "Whoever does not love does not know God, because God is love" (1 John 4:8).

If at our core we fail to come into agreement with God, who is love, we enter forever onto the path of blame and false evaluations. God is the first one we blame.

This is the primary truth of life. If we miss this, all else becomes hazy and constricting. If at our core we fail to come into agreement with the God, who is love, we enter forever onto the path of blame and false evaluations. God is the first one we blame. We follow the path of Adam in declaring, "The woman you put here with me— she gave me some fruit from the tree, and I ate it" (Gen. 3:12), in essence saying, "YOU ARE THE PROBLEM, GOD!" It is *Your* fault. I *knew* You were hard and unfair, so I acted as I did. From this point on we set ourselves on the road to perpetual blame and finger-pointing.

As we believe regarding the Author of Life, so we become in our actions toward others and ourselves. Self-reproach and condemnation are simply blame turned inward. Whether toward others or ourselves, blame starts with our perception of God. Our faith in God will either make us very much better or very much worse. If we think of ourselves as religious, yet

When we see, all criticism and reproach falls away—and we are free to love.

our God is hard and unfair, our light is actually darkness. Thus Jesus said, "If then the light within you is darkness, how great is that darkness!" (Matt. 6:23).

So when we blame and point the finger, at others or ourselves, we do not yet *see.* When we *see,* all criticism and reproach falls away—and we are free to love. That is, we are free to now take as our primary purpose in life the task of helping others feel loved, accepted, and forgiven. Only those who think they see, yet live in darkness, receive rebuke from the Lord. Prophets have always saved their anger for the religious hypocrite.

Jesus also had much to say to hypocrites, yet He was known as a friend of sinners, often asking of those who were crushed in spirit, "What do you want Me to do for you?" "Lord," they would answer, "we want our sight." Then, Jesus would have compassion on them. He would touch their eyes and immediately they received their sight and followed Him (Matt. 20:32–34).

But of those who chose to deliberately stay blind in their faulty vision of God, He would only say, "You hypocrite, first take the plank out of your own eye, and then you will see clearly to remove the speck from your brother's eye" (Matt. 7:5).

THE SCHOOL OF CHRIST

So what will you be doing when you are fulfilling your part of a healthy relationship? What will your family and friends see you doing that is different? How will you be able to tell this person noticed? If I had that video camera running in your house, what would I notice? How is that different from the way you have handled this situation recently, or in the past? Why not begin to do it now and observe what happens—any changes in your interactions with others. Then remember to do more of what works on purpose, looking to God for guidance and patience. In so doing you will begin to truly see. First, you will see that God is love, and His intention for you is perfect in design and implementation. God wastes nothing. Nothing! Problems are simply that . . . problems. They are the building blocks of your instruction in the school of Christ. Second, you will discover, again and again, that the ride of life is not to be feared but embraced. The Master has uniquely entered in to take every twist and turn, every up and down, and weave it into the tapestry of your physical existence, developing you into a mature son or daughter of God—and in the process you are mastering life.

Key Points and Action Steps for Personal Application

KEY POINT 1

Most of the problems you encounter are actually a combination of observable events. When you stand apart from your life and see these moments with a bird's-eye view, you discover a rich interplay of circumstances. The actions, reactions, and counteractions to so many of life's problems *can* become more clearly understood. God's design for your life includes all of these possibilities, weaving them into your experiences to accomplish His purpose.

➤ Action Step 1

- It is God's intention for you to succeed—but keep in mind that His definition of success may be different than yours—and His is the only one that counts. You can bring yourself in agreement with this intention when your intention is for others to succeed—and you deliberately work toward that end. If the other person is not very likable, keep in mind that you have not always been very likable from God's point of view. Make a choice to stop focusing on other persons as problems. Instead recognize the problem as the problem.
- On the scale below, with ten meaning you are a strong part of God's team in bringing about positive change in your interactions with others, and one meaning you are going to wait for the other person to change, where would you say you are today?

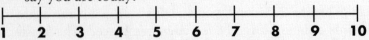

- As you move up this scale, how will you be adjusting your actions and reactions?
- As you do, what do you notice that is different with the interaction?

- Look for what works better than what you were doing previously—and do more of it. Remember, God is as actively involved in his or her life as He is in yours—whether this individual realizes it or not. Trust this new perception to continue working toward a healthier outcome. Write down in your notebook what occurs when you are more in agreement with God's plan for successful interactions. Continue to develop this skill with other interactions and relationships.

KEY POINT 2

Whenever you do not enjoy the true freedom of simply loving others, it is because of your faulty understanding of God. "Whoever does not love does not know God, because God is love" (1 John 4:8). This is the primary truth of life. When you forget this, or live as if it is not so, relationships become strained. At whatever point you fail to come into agreement with the God who is love, you will enter onto the path of blame and false evaluations. As you believe in your heart regarding the Author of Life, so you become in your actions toward yourself and others.

➤ Action Step 2

- It is your responsibility as God's person to remove the barriers to God's purpose to reveal His love. You do this by making yourself available to create, as much as it lies within you to do so, a more balanced and healthy environment in your home, in the church, and in the world. This will be an environment where persons *feel* loved, accepted, and forgiven. Each time you actively choose to be used by God to create such an environment, God's purpose will naturally form within you and around you.
- This week choose to view yourself as God's peace in difficult situations and relationships. What will your family and friends see you doing that is different when they are feeling loved, accepted, and forgiven by you?
- How will you be able to tell they have noticed?

- If I had that video camera running in your house, what would I notice?
- How is this different from the way you have handled this situation recently or in the past?

As you do this, observe what happens—any changes in your interactions with others. Then remember to do more of what works on purpose, looking to God for guidance and patience. In so doing, you will begin to see what Jesus meant when He said, "God blesses those who work for peace, for they will be called the children of God" (Matt. 5:9 NLT).

part two

Supporting God's Program for Others

chapter eleven

Supporting the Work of God's Spirit

In the very place that the enemy wounds us, once we are healed, we are given the power to heal others.

RICK JOYNER

Mastering life is the pathway to service. Service is the pathway to mastering life.

C. A. KOLLAR

Throughout this book I have been suggesting that each of us needs a personal change in focus, a shift from problems to solutions, so we can get on track. Life is the education, and the Holy Spirit is the Teacher. The following thoughts have formed each chapter and help to support our decisions and actions as we continue in the process of mastering life.

1. Your imagination is a fundamental resource. It must be used to create a new picture of your life by unlocking a vision of your life *without* the problem, deliberately creating a new vision of your future, and getting on track toward living that vision today. You can now begin to trust in God's intention and purpose during experiences that would once have caused great distress. Although this initially seems to be a mystery, Christ is being formed in you. You are developing the mind of Christ, the ability to see options and possibilities in the midst of the storm. But it takes the proper use of your God-given imagination.

2. You are the expert on your life, and you can learn how to intentionally come into agreement with God. This acceptance of personal responsibility will put you into the very heart of the transforming design of the Holy Spirit. You can create a vision of your future where you are taking greater action to solve your own problem. The goal is to initiate a pattern for future success—rather than focusing on past failures. Remember, vague goals are hard to visualize and even harder to accomplish. Specific goals will provide for you a sense of how you will know when you get there.

3. From time to time you will get stuck. Your problems need not represent symptoms of deeper dysfunctions. Rather, they more often represent the confines of your present perceptions—the limits of your neural pathways. You are created to have access into God's thought patterns—the mind of Christ.

4. Change is inevitable, and you can seize the opportunity to change in a way that leads toward new solutions, rather than toward a continuation of old or present problems. As you see this, you will discover that nothing is quite so ordinary and obvious as it first appeared. Indeed, God is found in the obvious and the ordinary. You are being rewritten by His love.

5. Although your problems may be complex, solutions need not be. As you listen and focus more on God's intention rather than the "rattles of the ride," you will learn to stop doing what is not working and start doing more of what works. Shifting your perspective in this way will help you discover how good or better things happen, how you can continue to have these good things happen, and how to build upon them. Your strengths will be utilized to encourage these "better" times to happen more often.

6. Your life has been touched by God. As you come into agreement with what God is already doing, His intention becomes the key to your life. In becoming aware and in agreement with His intention, you will begin to recognize His writing, grace, and design—which is infinitely greater

than anything you now perceive. Therefore, your perceptions of life's experiences must be critiqued in view of God's intention.

7. As you get deliberately involved in the development of your own life, you will begin to see the change. You cannot help but grow in Christ if you will seriously pay attention. You need to be willing to learn, to see what God is doing each day, to be trained by Him, and to apply these lessons in your various roles and responsibilities.

8. As you visualize your life without the dominance of present and past problems, you develop a new perception; you see yourself doing something different—you are seeing your life without the problem. With this new perspective you will discover that the problems that are now holding you back were not always present—nor are they always happening now. Finding these exceptions help to reveal your strengths and capabilities—and reveal what to do next.

9. As you start to behave in ways that actually work, you will begin to do more of the same on purpose—observing what is working and doing it deliberately. Learning how to slow down your reactive impulse and becoming more purposeful in your approach to life and decision making is essential to staying on track. Remember to "pause, praise, ponder, and plan."

10. Your actions will more often invite cooperation from others rather than defensiveness as you recognize the problem as the problem, not any individual—including yourself. Your responsibility is to remove the barriers to God's purposes and intentions. You will create a loving environment where you and your family can become healthy and feel loved. Health then opens the door to new possibilities to grow and be built up in love.

YOUR PERSONAL TRAINER

Is there a way to apply this ongoing instruction through God's Spirit to encourage others? How can we utilize our personal training from the Master to support those around us? There are some who feel this is an easy task—they simply give advice. Actually, I believe it is quite difficult. Consider how unique your training is. It is specifically tailored to your present level of understanding and your willingness to grow. This is why *only* the Holy Spirit can truly be your teacher—leading you into all the truth about your life. Remember, the apostle John wrote, "You do not need anyone to teach you . . . . His anointing teaches you about all things" (1 John 2:27). To bring His lessons to you, God uses His Word, individual teachers in and out of the church, all of life's wonders and tragedies, and your awareness of His presence in the "ordinary" present moment. Your education is the ultimate in "home" schooling. There is no such thing as one-size-fits-all instruction. The Holy Spirit is your "Personal Trainer" and your course of training will not fit any other human being on the face of the earth. So, what is it that we all have in common with others? Primarily one thing—we are all on the same "ride."

GETTING THE TRAIN ON TRACK

Visualize for a moment a train on a track. The engine is pulling one passenger car, and following after the passenger car is a caboose. The engine represents the power of the train. It depicts God's intention for your life—His desire to personally train you—to guide and help you learn from life. The passenger car is where the travelers stay to ride from one location to another. It depicts your choice regarding whether or not you will trust and rely upon God's intention or choose to "travel" to a different destination. It will remind you that you make this choice every moment of every day—a choice to focus toward the engine, that is, God's intended solution, or toward the caboose. The caboose is where the engineers live. It characterizes your emotional life, since we so often "live" in our emotions.

As you know, your emotions change—sometimes quite swiftly. The caboose (your emotions) *cannot* pull the train, but it will follow along once the engine starts moving forward—your actions resulting in the new emotion. Yet, the train can only move forward through the proper use of its engine, that is, when you choose to trust the intention of the life God has given and His personal training for your life. Forward motion ceases when you choose to trust in your ever-changing emotions rather than God's intention.

The track represents the process you will take to reach your destination. It reveals the way by showing your step-by-step progress as you move out from under the weight of personal problems.

Of course this train also needs a track and a destination. The track represents the process you will take to reach your destination. It reveals the way by showing your step-by-step progress as you move out from under the weight of personal problems. As the train moves ahead it also reveals your improvement and growth. Finally, the destination is what you see as you specifically imagine your life when problems no longer dominate you.

SUPPORTING THE WORK OF GOD'S SPIRIT

As we progress along the track we will find other passengers. They are on the same train with us whether they are aware of it or not—or, for that matter, whether we realize it or not. How can we support them in their journey? Not, I believe, with our "profound" advice. Their experience of life is so unique, their training so personal. At best our counsel flows out of our own experience of the journey. At worst it proceeds from pride and arrogance. In either case, it often fails to recognize the uniqueness of the individual we are trying to help.

I once considered writing a book entitled, "Why do Christians kill their wounded?" Perhaps too harsh a statement, I nevertheless all too regularly see professing Christians reinjure those who have been hurt—stabbing them in the open wound with the sword of "Truth." These wounds of discouragement or anxiety, hopelessness or fear, are reopened by well-meaning believers who "know" God's Word. They use this powerful two-edged sword like a child with a scalpel.

Never forget that this is the sword of the High Priest and its purpose is the same as that of the priests of ancient Israel. Taking the sacrifice, placing it on the altar, and wielding this razor-sharp sword, the priest would cut the sacrifice open—revealing its inward parts to God. So also, Jesus our High Priest takes the sword of His Spirit, the Word of God, and we are laid bare and exposed to the One before whom we will either stand or fall. As the writer to the Hebrews explains, "For the Word of God is living and active. Sharper than any double-edged sword, it penetrates even to dividing soul and spirit, joints and marrow; it judges the thoughts and attitudes of the heart" (Heb. 4:12).

> **The Master Gardener can expertly prune away dead branches that may otherwise hinder the fruitfulness of the plant. In the hands of imperfect humanity its danger is explicit—cutting at wounds that the Master is seeking to heal in His time.**

Just as the human brain is far more powerful than we realize, so also is God's written Word. In the hands of a Master Physician, it can cut away that which is diseased, so that the body may live. In the hands of a Master Gardener the Word can expertly prune away dead branches that may otherwise hinder the fruitfulness of the plant. In the hands of imperfect humanity its danger is explicit—cutting at wounds that the Master is seeking to heal in His time. Apart from the proclamation of the prophet, or a skilled biblical counselor, its purpose is to help us examine ourselves—not others. And if this is the case with God's Word, how much more our own advice.

Job learned this as he questioned the counsel of his "comforters." "Job replied to the LORD: 'I know that you can do all things; no plan of yours can be thwarted. You asked, "Who is this that *obscures my counsel without knowledge?*" Surely I spoke of things I did not understand, things too wonderful for me to know. You said, "Listen now, and I will speak; I will question you, and you shall answer me." My ears had heard of you but now my eyes have seen you. Therefore I despise myself and repent in dust and ashes'" (Job 42:1–6, italics added).

What a danger! To obscure God's counsel without knowledge! We easily give ready advice, speaking of things too wonderful for us to know about God's children. Rather, we should start with dust and ashes. Then perhaps we will begin to see beyond the log in our own eye—if such is even possible in this lifetime. Often, our best efforts to help amount to little more than words piled on top of one another. Most advice given or received is rarely helpful, and may even weary the one receiving it. Even when the words are good, they may not be timely. Why is this? It is because we are not called to simply give advice, but to support the work of God's Spirit in each life that we encounter. We are to speak the truth in love. What is the truth, and how do we present it lovingly? The apostle Paul wrote, ". . . speaking the truth in love, we will in all things grow up into him who is the Head, that is, Christ. From him the whole body, joined and held together by every supporting ligament, grows and *builds itself up in love,* as each part does its *work*" (Eph. 4:15–16, italics added). Is this not how we grow together within the body of Christ? We "build" one another up in love.

> **We are not called to simply give advice, but to support the work of God's Spirit in each life that we encounter.**

It has been said that whatever is not given away is lost. I would add this thought: Love is truly born when given away; love not given is lost. God is Love and His love gave birth to the universe. Also, this Divine Love, when placed within a single human spirit, brought forth humanity. So it was through Adam, and now through the second Adam, Jesus. Love has given birth to a restored and resurrected humanity—the body of Christ. By its nature love always multiplies itself in others. The entire universe resonates with this single truth. To act against it is to deny ourselves. In the midst of darkness, Love clearly declares itself. Even while a damaged human soul seeks in its agony to suppress Truth, it still hungers for Love. As we grow and mature in Christ we begin to recognize this essential fact about Love—we must support others in their journey.

> **Love is truly born when given away; love not given is lost.**

We are members of the body of Christ, and a unique part of the human family. Each day we are surrounded by those who have within themselves the potential to live as sons and daughters of God, to someday stand with Christ and inhabit eternity—or to dwell forever in eternal darkness. Our actions toward such persons, and our responses to them, will either support or hinder this process. How we treat one another has everlasting significance.

Again, we are to speak the truth in love and thereby grow up into Christ. If we do not love, we have no truth to speak. In Him we grow together, building ourselves up in love, as we each do our work. This is how we grow—we grow together. We "build" one another up in love. This takes place naturally as we each "do our work." This phrase comes from the word *energeia*, describing what has been effective within us. The King James Version of the Bible characterizes this as "effectual working." The New American Standard Bible refers to it as "proper working." It means we give to others what only we can give. We give what we have now begun to see, as well as the process that led to our ability to see. This is what we offer to others. So, how can we utilize our personal training from the Master to support others? We can support this process in them. Your personal training will give you the ability to help others discover God as their "Personal Trainer"—and therefore to come more naturally into agreement with their own purpose in life. This is infinitely more valuable than advice.

YOUR STORY, NOT HERS

Sometimes we can feel so helpless. We may try to fix things for others—only creating more frustration. The key is to trust the Master—not only through your experiences but also through theirs. I am reminded of another wonderful story from C. S. Lewis's Narnia series. In *The Horse and His Boy* there was a spoiled, young princess named Aravis, who runs away from her home and country to avoid a marriage that had been prearranged for her by her father. To escape, she drugged a servant girl, who was then mistaken for Aravis—thus giving her the time and opportunity to steal away. When she recounted this story to some companions on her journey she is asked, "And what happened to the girl—the one you drugged?" To this she replied coolly, "Doubtless she was beaten for sleeping late... But she was a tool and a spy of my stepmother's. I am very glad they should beat her."

Later in the story Aslan, who, as you remember, is both a powerful lion and a type of Jesus Christ, scratches the back of this arrogant princess. She believes that her narrow escape was from the jaws of an ordinary lion—not recognizing that it was an encounter with her Creator. (How much of life is like this?) Near the end of the story we find a repentant and wiser princess who now sees Aslan for who He is. He says to her,

> "Draw near, Aravis my daughter. See! My paws are velveted. You will not be torn this time."
>
> "This time, sir?" said Aravis.
>
> "It was I who wounded you," said Aslan. "I am the only Lion you met in all your journeyings. Do you know why I tore you?"
>
> "No, sir."
>
> "The scratches on your back, tear for tear, throb for throb, blood for blood, were equal to the stripes laid on the back of your stepmother's slave because of the drugged sleep you cast upon her. You needed to know what it felt like."
>
> "Yes sir. Please—"
>
> "Ask on, my dear," said Aslan.
>
> "Will any more harm come to her by what I did?"
>
> "Child," said the Lion, "I am telling you your story, not hers. No-one is told any story but their own."

From this story I believe two important points emerge. First, in all our "journeyings" our encounters are always with Jesus Christ, either intentionally, as we commune with him in prayer and praise, or as we live out His purposeful design and intention for each of His children. God is your Personal Trainer—sometimes painfully so! The second is equally important: We are only told our own story. "No-one is told any story but their own." Stop trying to fix others. Your efforts will only result in increased disappointment and may actually lead to some pretty sticky situations. When we seek to support other persons in counseling, what we are actually supporting is the writing of the Spirit in their lives. The key, though, is to trust the Master of your life and *their* life.

SUPPORTIVE HINTS

To do this we must remain faithful to the process God has already begun within them. Part 1 offered numerous facets of this process. Let me now reword these from the perspective of supporting others, and also present some hints as to how to stay on track while you do. Please keep in mind, our goal here is not to extend professional therapy but rather to offer supportive counsel. We are *supporting* God's work in their lives. If you feel you are in "over your head," the most loving thing you can do is to listen graciously, offer emotional support, and refer the person to a pastoral counselor or a professional Christian counselor. When you do feel you can help, remember to:

- **Help them to use their imagination in a supportive way.** Seek to encourage them to *see* beyond their immediate problem and to create a new *vision* for their future.
- **Remember, it is their life.** Each life is unique. You are not the expert on any life other than your own. When they see their own solutions, they will be more likely to succeed.
- **They are most likely stuck.** Do not look for deeper dysfunctions, for you will find what you are looking for. Seek instead to learn what they want—not what they do not want.
- **Keep in mind, they are always changing.** An expectation of change will produce change.
- **Their problems may seem complex, but the solution need not be.** Rather than focusing on what is causing the problem, consider what is stopping the people you are seeking to help from noticing solutions.
- **They have already been touched by God.** Learn to trust what God is already doing in these lives. Support the work that God has already begun. It does not begin with you.
- **Encourage them to get involved in the ride of their lives.** Seek to discover ways that will assist the people you are

trying to help to become willing participants in the process of God's personal training.

- **When their problems are solved, how will they know?** Help them to look for clues to when the problem is not happening.
- **Help them to do what works on purpose.** Encourage them to critique their perceptions—hopefully comparing them to God's intention. Remember, a change in meaning results in a change in the memory of an experience.
- **Remember, the problem is the problem.** Help them to imagine ways they can remove barriers to God's purposes and intentions, such as blaming, and begin to work to create a more loving environment.

Utilizing these suggestions is the focus of the final chapter.

chapter twelve

Designing a Supportive Climate

Whatever we learn to do, we learn by actually doing it: Men come to be builders, for instance, by building, and harp players by playing the harp. In the same way, by doing just acts, we come to be just; by doing self-controlled acts, we learn to be self-controlled; and by doing brave acts, we become brave.

ARISTOTLE

So how do we put the suggestions from the previous chapter into practice? How can we find a way to be supportive of God's intention for others? It would be helpful to have a design or pattern. This design should be easy to remember. What is required is a way to visualize the design so as to remember what to do next when offering support—to help create an environment where someone can get back on track with God. What can we do that supports their story and will also help us know what to do at each point when we are offering this support? The following diagram presents a biblical, joyful,

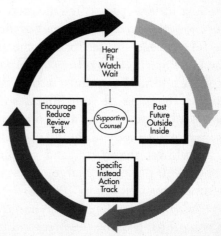

creative, hopeful, expectant, and commonsense way to do this very thing.

HEAR, FIT, WATCH, AND WAIT

You may not believe yourself to be a counselor, but as much as our lives touch others, we all should know how to give support. We especially need to discover how to assist the Holy Spirit. We learn by doing—and that is the purpose of life in a nutshell. But when we offer supportive counsel it helps to have a plan. Without one, offering support may become a frustrating experience. At the top of the supportive counsel diagram are the words, "hear," "fit," "watch," and "wait." They represent the first part of the process in giving help. Each word opens up a thought or concept, and together they reveal the first responsibility of the listener—to listen!

Hear

"The first duty of love is to listen" (Paul Tillach).

The apostle James wrote, "Everyone should be quick to listen [and] slow to speak" (James 1:19). If we obey James's exhortation, we will learn more about the one we are listening to. We will communicate acceptance to and connection with that person. If we do not listen, most of what we seek to accomplish will be fruitless because the one coming to us for support will not feel that his or her experiences and emotions have been heard and felt.

Five little words—"Tell me more about that"—can open the door for others to express a part of their life to you. This is a wonderful privilege—to see for a moment into the creative activity of the Holy Spirit. That other soul represents God's most priceless creative effort. The psalmist wrote, "When I look at the night sky and see the work of your fingers—the moon and the stars you have set in place—what are mortals that you should think of us, mere humans that you should care for us? For you made us only a little lower than God, and you crowned us with glory and honor. You put us in charge of everything you made, giving us authority over all things"(Ps. 8:3–6 NLT).

As a navy chaplain I often had the opportunity to go to sea. It is hard to describe the breathtaking beauty of a clear, crisp, moonless night in the North Atlantic. I recall one evening, standing near the back of the ship, looking forward. The large seven-story-high superstructure in the center of the topside deck was invisible due to the darkness. When I looked at it, all I could see was darkness, which *was* the superstructure, swaying slowly back and forth. It was outlined by the thickest blanket of brilliant stars I had ever seen. Indeed, the sky was filled with such majesty that even the ocean reflected the stars. We were literally "flying" in a sea of stars. "When I look at the night sky and see the work of your fingers—the moon and the stars you have set in place ..." All of this is but the "work of God's fingers" yet it inspires such awe. What are we mere humans that God should care about us? The answer, "For you made us only a little lower than God, and you crowned us with glory and honor...." I try to remember that each human being that my life touches—even if only for a moment—should inspire more awe than I felt on that moonless night so many years ago! So, when we "hear" their stories, we are hearing the unfolding of God's intention.

When we hear others' stories, we are hearing the unfolding of God's intention.

Fit

When you seek to support others, you have the unique opportunity to enter the world of the one you are listening to. When you do, it is important to show that you understand their concerns. To demonstrate this understanding is what I mean by "fit." The prophet Amos wrote, "Do two walk together unless they have agreed to do so?" (Amos 3:3). In hearing, and now in fitting, we simply want to walk together with individuals as they begin to move forward with God's intention. We "rejoice with those who rejoice, and mourn with those who mourn" (Rom. 12:15). In this way we show them that we are with them when they are rejoicing (light emotions) or mourning (intense or heavy emotions). Our response needs to "fit" theirs. Remember to pay attention to both your verbal and nonverbal responses. It is better if your words and tone of voice respond to the voice of the one you are assisting. Even your physical posture can support this "fit." If the individual is sitting back, relaxed, with his legs crossed, eventually you can take a similar position. When he or she is anxious and concerned, leaning forward, you can join together in that position—not being anxious, but as a nonanxious presence, being with them in their fears. By being with them in their hopeless or anxious world, we can also help to create the potential for a hopeful world with less fear—highlighting the meaningfulness of this newly forming hope.

Watch

Look for evidence of God's activity in the person's life. Watch for any indication of exceptions to the problem, any grace events where the individual has successfully dealt with similar problems, any writing of the Spirit when God has entered the story but the person has not appreciated the significance. Just place this information on the "back burner." It will help you later as you look for solutions. You must listen attentively if you are going to catch the clues that God already has in place.

Wait

At some point, after a season of gracious listening, the individual will shift from retelling past concerns to a present request for support. This shift offers you an invitation to join in the conversation. I strongly encourage you to wait for this open door. It may come in the form of simple silence—hopefully looking up to you for help. Or perhaps the person will look down, shaking his or her head, wondering if there is any hope. What you say next will set the tone for the rest of your conversation. At this moment you want to proceed to the second set of words on the circle diagram.

PAST, FUTURE, OUTSIDE, AND INSIDE

Think about how you gather information. It is often by asking questions. Questions can also lead us into seeing a situation in a new way. Remember the picture of the lady? As you considered the picture, I asked you what you saw. This simple question led to a new discovery. It also resulted in your brain making a new neural connection. If you were to look back right now you would still see both faces quite easily; the "connection" is still firmly a part of who you are.

So how are we to utilize questions in supportive counseling? The answer proceeds from both a simple commonsense discussion with the individual and an appreciation of God's intention for their lives. The thoughts that formed each chapter were given to you to encourage an appreciation of God's intention for you. This understanding must now inform your use of some basic questions. It is not the question that is significant.

> **We all possess the ability to imagine a future solution when the problem is solved.**

Rather, each question helps to move those you are seeking to help through a "doorway" into a more solution-focused way of living. Getting through the door is the goal of this stage—not the question.

For example, the Bible tells us that our faith gains us access to God's grace (Rom. 5:2). In a similar fashion, our *questions* gain, for those we are supporting, access to a vision of life where their problems do not dominate them. We want them to discover what that life will look like and how this will make a difference. What will be happening when they are on track toward this kind of life? (Remember the "train.") What will this track look like? What will the first step look like on this track? How about the second and third steps? What will they need to do to stay on track? What part of this is happening already? Keep in mind, God has a purpose for giving us an imagination. With it we all possess the ability to imagine a future solution when the problem is solved. This is an incredible resource, often underutilized or used in the wrong way. Even though the problem is still dominating their lives, a solution is open to our investigation. We want to support a gradually clearer picture of it. Now, in this second part of the process of offering supportive counsel, let us look at four doorways—and the questions that will take you, and those you seek to help, through them.

Past

After being invited in, you may discover that something has already happened that will reveal some minor improvement in the problem they have just shared with you. So far this has not been viewed as meaningful. Therefore, this first doorway assumes possible change in the past and is curious about what it may be. Since God is always active we should not be surprised when He has already placed "clues" of possible change or improvement into their lives. I recall one fellow who I was talking to who felt depressed. After hearing his story, and being invited into the conversation, I asked him what he had noticed that had been better the past few days. He told me that he had gotten out of his apartment more. He was not just going to work and going home. I thought that was great, and I told him so. Then I asked him how he had been able to get himself to do that.

My first question had opened a door to a small exception to his depression. It seemed as if I was simply curious, but I assumed the possibility of the exception. This offered a potential to create a solution. In response to my second "curious" question he informed me that he had just decided to drive right by his exit home and go bowling. While there he met some folks from a local church and had a pretty good time. Now, I would not have known about this if I had not asked. At this point I asked a couple of clarifying questions that helped to draw more attention to this change from being depressed "all" the time. For example, "How do you account for this change in your attitude? Is it different for you to do these things? What will you have to continue to do to feel better more often? How will you do that?" Well, you see the point.

These are all simple questions that keep us peeking through the door at what this exception looks like, and what life will look like *when* (not if) it happens more often. I am not suggesting that you ask one question after another in a shotgun approach, but rather to ask these "curious" or "clarifying" questions in a very matter-of-fact way—because you care—and because you are interested. Then allow yourself to have a normal conversation based on this new view of reality. Basically, we are just wondering what this exception looks like, and what life will be like *when* (not if) more of this happens. Is this a good thing? How will it happen more? Again, the questions flow naturally from being focused more on solutions in our own lives—more in agreement with our Personal Trainer. When we are, it is not too difficult to help others to get a glimpse of their lives in a similar fashion.

If this doorway has opened up new possibilities, I proceed to the third component of the supportive counsel process (the "six o'clock" position). Of course, this first door will not always bring forth the response hoped for. At times, no past change will be reported. The person is not able to see beyond the problem to recognize anything that may reveal an exception. There may *be* some exceptions, but right now they are so focused on the present problem that they cannot see them. When this happens your next question will simply turn the handle on a different door. Keep in mind, each doorway has but one purpose—to lead to the third part of the supportive counsel process. When it is effective, only one door is necessary.

> When we are focused more on solutions in our own lives, it is not too difficult to help others to get a glimpse of their lives in a similar fashion.

Future

The second door shifts the individual's perspective to a future focus. It helps them to project their faith to the future and to create a more hopeful expectation. One counselor asked questions such as "How would your life be different if you did not have this problem?" or "What would you do if you were well?" (Alfred Adler). Another asked, "If right now you had what you want, how do you imagine that your life would be different?" (William Glasser).

Although I prefer a stronger suggestion, that is, "what *will* be" rather than "what *would* be" different, I nevertheless appreciate the focus of these questions. God's Word is even more explicit. It tells us that a Christian has been made free from his or her old life and sin (1 Cor. 6:11) and that future health and spiritual growth are already complete! One of the most incredible statements in the Bible is the apostle Paul's words to the ancient Roman church. He wrote, "And we know that in all things God works for the good of those who love him, who have been called according to his purpose. For those God foreknew he also *predestined to be conformed to the likeness of his Son,* that he might be the firstborn among many brothers. And those he predestined, he also called; those he called, he also justified; those he justified, he also glorified" (Rom. 8:28–30, italics added).

We see that God wants us to view our future in Him as *already achieved.* This does not nullify our human freedom. Rather, it is through our decision to recognize Jesus as Lord, and the Holy Spirit as our Teacher, that our lives now come into agreement with His plan. The mystery is that God reclaims our past and then reveals that His intention was always unfolding—since the perfection of our lives has been open to His eyes from the beginning.

I said earlier that anxiety is a form of present or past fears that are being extended to the future. It represents a belief that the near or distant future will consist of nothing more than an extension of the present or past experience of uneasiness. This form of fear has a relational and spiritual origin. It was born in the Garden when Adam and Eve first hid from God (see Gen. 3:10). This same kind of fear has bound the entire human race—since all are hiding from God. There is in the world a "spirit of fear" that has not proceeded from the Creator (2 Tim. 1:7). It will culminate in hopelessness that makes our "hearts" sick. As Solomon wrote,

> **Most individuals who have lived through great sorrow, frustration, or fear in the past have an increasingly hopeless expectation for the future. This hopeless stance is like a self-fulfilling prophecy.**

"Hope deferred makes the heart sick, but a longing fulfilled is a tree of life" (Prov. 13:12). Hope is the antidote. Unhappily, most individuals who have lived through great sorrow, frustration, or fear in the past have an increasingly hopeless expectation for the future. This hopeless stance is like a self-fulfilling prophecy. As Job said, "What I feared has come upon me" (Job 3:25).

This intensifies the present difficulty by casting hopelessness to both past and future. Through supportive counseling, we can come into a more accurate awareness of God's view of the future where we are destined to be like Jesus. This new vision produces hope. Our view of the past takes on a new meaning as it increasingly is viewed as being an essential part of life. It becomes instructive rather than shameful, terrifying, or traumatic. We then begin to see new possibilities and potential solutions, which help us to more effectively deal with present problems.

In chapter 8 I asked you to consider what would happen if, while you were sleeping, a miracle took place. In it your problems were solved, but you were not aware that this miracle had occurred. I then wondered what you would notice the next day that revealed to you that the miracle had indeed happened. This question, and others like it, opens up an alternate reality of possibilities. Remember the Lotto winner from the same chapter? That conversation represented going through this "future" doorway. The purpose of subsequent questions was to clarify some of the responses.

For example, I could ask, "What else will be different when this miracle takes place?" "Tell me more about that." "What will you be doing differently when you are (doing the miracle)?" "What will you be doing differently when you are not (doing the problem)?" "What will your (family, spouse, child, and so forth) notice that is different about you when . . . ?" You get the point. As you can see, the emphasis is on what *will* be happening, not *would* be happening.

So, what actions or things will those you seek to help be doing differently? It is not the miracle question that is significant, but the hypothetical possibilities that it opens to the one responding. Another way of saying the same thing would be, "Let's step out in faith and say that our talking together has been helpful to you. How will you know it has been helpful?" Again, asking them to tell you more about that, and what will be different, helps to build upon this alternate possibility. Remember, as you encourage this "future" focus you will discover once again that it is quite a bit easier to act your way to a feeling rather than to feel your way to an action.

This is also true for children. A pretend question can be quite helpful. For example, "Let's pretend the (problem) is solved, and you are getting along better with (family, school children). What are you doing differently?" Also, the Scripture itself offers abundant opportunity for creating a "future" focus. Consider the following: "Set your minds on things above, not on earthly things. For you died, and your life is now hidden with Christ in God" (Col. 3:2–3). "I have been crucified with Christ and I no longer live, but Christ lives in me. The life I live in the body, I live by faith in the Son of God, who loved me and gave himself for me" (Gal. 2:20). "We were therefore buried with him through baptism into death in order that, just as Christ was raised from the dead through the glory of the Father, we too may live a new life" (Rom. 6:4). Each of these passages represents our death and new life in Christ. We could therefore ask, "If you died and lived again in Christ, and all the problems that we have been discussing today are gone, what will you observe that will prove to you that this new life has begun?"

Numerous passages point us in this direction. For example, "Rejoice in the Lord always. I will say it again: Rejoice! Let your gentleness be evident to all. The Lord is near. Do not be anxious about anything, but in everything, by prayer and petition, with thanksgiving, present your requests to God. And the peace of God, which transcends all understanding, will guard your hearts and your minds in Christ Jesus" (Phil. 4:4–7). This portion of Scripture could be followed by asking, "If a miracle happened this afternoon and you were no longer being controlled by anxieties, but rather had this peace of God, what will you notice that is different? Keep in mind that this miracle transcends your ability to understand it. What is the first thing you will notice that is different?" "What else?" "What will you be doing differently?"

How about the issue of spiritual warfare? Consider this: "No temptation has seized you except what is common to man. And God is faithful; he will not let you be tempted beyond what you can bear. But when you are tempted, he will also provide a way out so that you can stand up under it" (1 Cor. 10:13). Again, this Scripture could be followed by asking, "What will be the first sign to you that God is providing a way out from this problem?"

At times this second door may not bring the response hoped for either. Perhaps he or she is not able to see any possible hope for change—remaining firmly held in place by present perceptions. The third possible doorway will shift the perception once again. Thus far we have tried the past and the future. Now we will try looking outside—deliberately viewing the problem as the problem. Keep in mind, this doorway like the others has but one purpose—to lead to the third component of the process.

Outside

Remember the *Star Trek* story regarding the "alien entity" in chapter 10? It simply popped into my mind as I was thinking of ways I could deliberately put the problem "outside" of the couple. By doing so, they became partners in defeating this "outside" influence. It also prepared the way for them to cooperate with each other. They were united in a battle against the problem—to break out from its grip in their lives.

So also we know that our battle is with Satan, not with others or ourselves. The primary problem is outside of us. Therefore, Paul wrote, "Our struggle is not against flesh and blood, but against the rulers, against the authorities, against the powers of this dark world and against the spiritual forces of evil in the heavenly realms" (Eph. 6:12). The apostle even refers to the issue of sin as outside of us. "For sin, seizing the opportunity afforded by the commandment, deceived me, and through the commandment put me to death. . . . I do not understand what I do. For what I want to do I do not do, but what I hate I do. And if I do

The problem is not other people, or even ourselves, but the deceiving influence of evil acting subtly behind the curtain.

what I do not want to do, I agree that the law is good. As it is, *it is no longer I myself who do it, but it is sin living in me* . . . . Now if I do what I do not want to do, it is no longer I who do it, but it is sin living in me that does it" (Rom. 7:11, 15–17, 20, italics added).

Thus the problem is not other people, or even ourselves, but the deceiving influence of evil acting subtly behind the curtain. God wants us to be free from seeing the other person—spouse, child, family member, neighbor, coworker, or stranger—as the enemy or the problem. We can join together with God's Spirit and others to fight a common foe. Some questions that will help you to assist others to find this "outside" look include "If (the problem) is the enemy, how can you come together to defeat it?" or "When you are winning, what are you doing?" or "When was the last time you were under attack, but you didn't let (this problem) win? How did you do that?"

Sometimes people are simply getting beaten up by their problems. This reminds me of the story Billy Graham once told of the beaten and battered boxer. Bruised and bleeding he leans over to his trainer and says, "Please throw in the towel! This guy is killing me!" To this the trainer responded, "Oh, no, he's not. He's not even hitting you. He hasn't laid a glove on you!" To which the boxer replied, "Well then, I wish you'd watch that referee because *somebody* is sure hitting me!"

To these folks you might ask, "How long have you been getting beat up by (this problem)?" or "How long are you going to let (this problem) get the best of you?" or "When was the last time (this problem) tried to get the best of you, but you didn't let it? How did you do that?" Of course the problem can be anything from blame in relationships to a child's fear of the dark. Once again, if this third door does not bring the response hoped for, there is another yet to try. Perhaps they are so focused on the present problem that they cannot see any other possibilities. This is a hopeless and helpless stance. If that is the case, we want to maintain "fit" with this sense of hopelessness. The fourth door helps us to do just this. Keep in mind that this doorway, like the others, has but one purpose—to lead to the third process around the circle.

Inside

When those you are seeking to support are unable to discover any exceptions in the past, to envision life without the problem in the future, or to imagine the problem as outside of them, then you may want to take the conversation "inside." These are times when we "mourn with those who mourn" (Rom. 12:15). For a moment you agree with both their hopeless feeling—and maintain agreement with God's intention. To do so you can ask questions about how they have kept everything

> A change in perspective will in turn offer a change in the meaning of a situation.

from getting worse. For example, "It's amazing that you have been able to put up with this. How have you been able to manage?" When you ask this question you are asking them to go "inside" themselves and evaluate how they have been able to keep things from getting worse! Again, you could ask, "From what you say, it seems the problem is quite serious. How is it that things are not worse?" or "What are you doing to keep this situation from getting worse?"

This type of question ushers the person through a door that leads once again to possible solutions. It is amazing how quickly the conversation can change. You may ask, "What are you doing to manage when things are so bad?" Usually, at this point, they will remark upon something that has helped them to manage, even if they are just getting by. As you can see, an "exception" to the problem has just been displayed. Once they respond with any example or instance of how they have managed, or why things are not worse, you can curiously ask them to clarify this.

One way I have done this is to say something like, "How has that been helpful to you?" and "What will it take to make that happen more often?" You could also continue by asking, "As more of this happens, and things start to get better, what do you imagine yourself doing then?" Other questions I ask from time to time have been, "How did you come up with that idea?" or "How did you do that?" or "It seems to me that God is trying to do something to help. What are some of the signs that a little of that is happening right now?" Again, the questions naturally flow out of a fairly simply, commonsense approach to helping people see their situation from a new perspective. Keep in mind that this change in perspective will in turn offer a change in the meaning of the situation—and this is a change that can truly make a difference!

WHEN EVERY DOOR IS BLOCKED

As I said earlier, our purpose is not to extend professional counseling services but rather to offer support that helps persons get back on track. Sometimes nothing you try will help them see other possibilities. Exploring the future without a change may offer some assistance. For example, you might say, "If (the other person) does not change, what will you do?" This question helps them define what *they* will do that is within their control—even if the situation does not change immediately for the better. When nothing helps, and the individual is caught in despair or frustration, it will be tempting to begin offering advice. If God has given you wisdom in this area, by all means give it—but keep in mind the uniqueness of each person's journey. It has been said that it's easier to be wise for others than for ourselves (François, Duc de La Rochefoucauld). I try to keep this in mind.

One thing we *can* all offer is a sympathetic ear. But be careful with simplistic words of encouragement. At times when persons are in the midst of great personal testing and trial, our words of "encouragement" may have the opposite effect—actually frustrating the listener. The reason this happens is that their *ride* is so unique and the words tend to offer a more "packaged" approach. Even the Bible, as precious as it is, can have this effect when used in such a fashion. It has been said, "I would rather see a sermon than hear one." This is the priority of true support. Words are often too easy to give.

Let us keep this in mind with the one who is not able, at that moment, to remove their focus from the problem to see any other possibilities. We listen, offering a *nonanxious* presence. How can we do this? Because we trust the Master.

> I would rather see a sermon than hear one.

We are not trying to fix their lives—which would reveal a mistrust of God's program for their future. "For who are [we] to judge someone else's servant? To his own master he stands or

falls. *And he will stand, for the Lord is able* to make him stand"
(Rom. 14:4, italics added).

I recall the time I conducted a funeral for a navy commander
who had died suddenly of a heart attack. I did my best to comfort both family and friends. Then I watched as an elderly woman
came over to the widow. I was curious to see what she would do,
what condolences she would offer, or what words of wisdom and
advice she would give. To my amazement she simply sat quietly
next to her, gently placing her hand over the grieving wife's hand,
patting it tenderly, and *staying* with her for awhile. Without
speaking, she remained for many minutes. Her "presence" spoke
more eloquently than any words she could have offered at that
time. Eventually, this widow will *hear* words spoken by friends
and relatives. Yet on this day she *heard* the wisdom of an open
and compassionate heart—without words.

Never underestimate the power of just being *with* someone.
Over two hundred years ago William Cowper wrote, "God never
meant that man should scale the heavens by strides of human wisdom." Although Jesus was and is Wisdom in human form, it is
not the wisdom of Jesus that primarily draws the human soul—
it is Jesus Himself, His presence. How much more is this true of
you and me. Even when all the doors seem to be blocked to you,
they are in no way blocked to God's presence through you. In
such cases, we offer His *nonanxious* presence and proceed past
the third portion of the diagram directly to the final section on
encouraging feedback. More on this later.

SPECIFIC, INSTEAD, ACTION, AND ON TRACK

When a door has been opened and a shift in thinking from a problem focus to a solution focus has occurred, it is time to proceed
to the third part of the circle. This component has but one purpose—to further clarify this new vision of the solution. Much
time has already been spent with them in seeking to understand
their problem. You have listened with compassion and compre-
hension. Now you want to place the same effort into understanding the solution. *This can only occur by discussing it.* This
part of the process helps you to do just that.

Specific

Have you ever watched a mystery movie where a crime has been committed and the detective is gathering information by asking questions of the witness? What is the purpose of his questions? They help to clarify the memory of the one he is questioning. After asking a few fact-gathering questions, the detective begins to get a pretty clear picture of what the witness saw. The process continues with this individual giving ever clearer descriptions of the event. In this way, the detective's careful use of a few questions clarifies the memory of the witness—actually giving a clearer picture than he felt able to give at first.

As the detective seeks to clarify the memory of the event for the witness, so we are trying to clarify the initial "memory" of a solution—past, future, outside, or inside. What will he be doing specifically? What will he be saying? What will he be thinking? What will others be doing and saying? In this way the solution is developed one piece at a time. I would encourage you to ask questions such as, "Can you tell me more *specifically* how you and your husband will be communicating when you are doing this?" or "How *exactly* will you be doing this?" or "Tell me *precisely* how you will be doing this?"

> Our lives are not built upon what we must not or cannot do, but about who we *are* and what we *can* do in Christ.

Through this kind of discussion, a clearer picture has appeared. It has come from the imagination of the one you are seeking to support, and it was your love and patience that gave him the ability to develop it. It is from this growing picture of the solution that a direction will arise. With some encouragement you will support their initial first steps toward what they have described.

Instead

I am reminded of the saying, "Christians don't smoke, drink or chew, or hang around with those who do." So now we know what this Christian does not do, but what *does* he do? We want to keep in mind that our lives are not built upon what we must not or cannot do, but about who we *are* and what we *can* do in Christ. Our life in Christ gives us every reason to be optimistic, expectant, and hopeful.

So also, those we are seeking to offer support to usually tell us what they do *not* want, that is, their problems. We have now opened up a doorway to what they do want. Thus, if a wife was to say to you that she does not want to argue anymore with her husband, it is fruitless trying to envision *not* arguing. If you think of it, the only picture that really comes into the imagination is of the two of them arguing. Rather, we want to utilize the imagination to discover what she will be doing instead.

This word will help support a more hopeful and expectant outcome. I encourage you to be more concerned with the presence of something rather than the absence of something. This is what creates hope. This is what gives us something to look forward to. There is not enough darkness in the world to put out the light of one candle. Why? Because darkness is simply the absence of light, it has no actual substance. When a person continues to describe problems as what they do not want, they are stating a negative goal—it has no substance. This goal cannot be imagined. Unfortunately, what it often does is reinforce the problem. We want to support by helping them create and envision what they *will be doing instead*.

Action

I have never seen a Hollywood movie made, but I think when the shooting is getting ready to begin they say words something like, "Ready, places, action." What are they creating? They are producing a *moving* picture. The whole movie will be a description of action. So also, we do not want a still picture but a moving picture to form in the minds of those we are seeking to support. We want to encourage responses that describe their own actions or the actions of others.

> **We want a moving picture to form in the minds of those we are seeking to support.**

I suggest that you help them form this moving picture by asking some questions that simply begin with the word "how." For example, a husband who is willing to help his marriage get back on track, but who has been angry and unresponsive, could be asked, "How will you be showing your wife that you love her in a way that she will feel loved?" Perhaps he will respond by saying, "I will be hugging her and looking into her eyes more," or "I will be planning dates more often and I'll be treating her with respect." Perhaps he will even say, "I'll be helping with the housework by doing the laundry and vacuuming." (Now we're back into miracles!) As you can see, these responses describe actions. In reply to a "how" question, this husband is describing what he will be doing, and is therefore creating a clearer picture of a possible goal. Again, "How will you be doing this?" will create a picture of action.

On Track

Once through a door, we want to help others clarify their initial description by asking them to describe what they will be doing more "specifically." Then we help them discover what they actually want by describing what they will be doing "instead." We also want this to be an action picture, so we ask "how" they will do this. Now we want to bring this description into the present. We do not want them imagining this action as something they will do eventually. Rather, we want to help them describe this potential solution as something they can get on track with right away.

If the person you are trying to help wants to strengthen his or her marriage, you could ask, "When you are on track to strengthening your marriage, what will you be doing differently?" This type of question helps persons to see what they can do right now. You do not want potential solutions to be so distant that they are of no practical use. Thus, we use questions to create a more immediate track to that future hope. For example you could ask, "What will be the first sign that you are on track to getting a little better?" or "As you continue to do these things, will you see yourself as being on track to getting what you wanted when you came to see me?" You could also imagine the train illustration to recognize movement along the track. Remember that this movement will reveal forward progress in reaching their clearly defined goals.

In chapter 2 I gave you a tool called a "tracking scale" to help you do this very thing. This would be a good time to utilize this tool in supportive counseling as well. The scale helps us to organize and visualize the picture and clarify the direction we are going. In this way, those you are helping will be able to visualize both where they are at the present time, as well as where they will be going. The answers to the scale are entirely based on their view of themselves. You can offer support no matter where they place themselves on the scale. Again, the basic form of a tracking scale is this: "On a scale from one to ten, where ten means how you want things to be, and one means the worst things have been, where would you say you are right now?" As we saw in chapter 2, you can use these scales to help others assess their level of commitment to a relationship, organize specific goals, appraise self-concept and self-esteem, clarify communication, encourage hopefulness, and determine a willingness to work toward solutions, to name just a few possible goals. Remember to offer this approach humbly, letting the one you are seeking to help know that this is simply a tool that has helped you clarify your own choices.

In this way we support life's journey. So far you have listened, maintained fit, watched for clues, waited for an invitation, walked through a doorway, and once in, you have helped the persons you are supporting to clarify a new vision of their situation. Now you will want to have a clear plan for finishing the conversation on an upbeat note that encourages them, reduces their fears, reviews what they have seen, and gives them a clear and uncomplicated way of continuing this process on their own.

ENCOURAGE, REDUCE, REVIEW, AND TASK

The final component of supportive counseling includes offering encouraging feedback. (This is also the section you proceed to directly if all of the doors in section two were temporarily blocked.) We want to develop an environment that offers them *hope*, that is, a *H*opeful, *O*ptimistic, *P*ositive, and *E*xpectant climate. Therefore, instead of feeling overwhelmed due to openly discussing their problems, those you support will feel more positive and expectant of change. For example, someone who thought he was doing everything wrong may respond to your encouragement by saying, "Well, I guess I'm not as bad as I thought I was," or "I'm doing something right after all." Again, God's *intention* should inspire such a response. Once again, keep in mind what God said through the prophet Jeremiah, "'For I know the plans I have for you,' declares the LORD, 'plans to prosper you and not to harm you, plans to give you hope and a future'" (Jer. 29:11). This hope creates a sense of expectancy, a belief that the future can really be better than the past.

Encourage

I advise you to limit the length of time you spend offering supportive counsel. Thirty minutes to an hour should be sufficient. Too little time and they may not believe you have heard them. Too much time and both of you may become fatigued. Once it seems to you that they feel heard, and you have helped them to develop a fairly clear moving picture of a potential solution, then it is time to come to a close. In my professional practice I will often take a break for a couple of minutes to form my thoughts, and then return with some suggestions. It gives a clear line between the counseling session and the feedback. In this way my client knows it is now time to listen to me.

In the case of supportive counseling, an actual break may be too awkward. I suggest that you seek to draw such a line in another way. This can be done by saying something like, "Why don't we pause now for a moment so I can give you some feedback?" This

Limit the length of time you spend offering supportive counsel.

is not a complete break, but rather a shift in the flow of the discussion. The first shift came when you were invited in. Now you are shifting from the heart of the conversation to the closing thoughts. These closing thoughts should begin with any legitimate compliments or praise that you can offer. Even the smallest amount of effort on their part needs to be encouraged.

Often those you are trying to help did not initially view their efforts as meaningful. For example, to a parent who had expressed deep concern to me regarding her daughter, and who in counseling now saw a possible new course of action, I said, "I am very impressed by the love and support you obviously have for your daughter. It is clear that you deeply love her. Just wanting some help demonstrates how much you want to encourage her, and I congratulate you on your persistence." Now this may seem like I was coming on a little strong, but persons who have just opened up their souls tend to feel vulnerable. We want them to know that we appreciate their openness and honesty. I often start with the words "I am impressed." From there it does not take much to convey your respect and reconfirm your support.

Actually, praising this mom also accomplished two other purposes. First, it helped to *normalize* the problem. There are times when she may feel quite alone with her frustrations. She even wonders if there could be something wrong with her. She may think, "Perhaps I am the only one who has a problem like this." In offering a little praise and encouragement, I was reminding her of Paul's words that no temptation has taken hold of her except what is common to us all (see 1 Cor. 10:13).

Second, it reinforces personal responsibility. I wanted to point out what she had done that had been good. I always want to give all credit for any perceived changes to those I support. Whatever good has happened is due to their efforts, and more importantly, because God wants them to succeed. You will discover that your honest praise and compliments allow them to not only enjoy their efforts, but also encourages them to continue to take responsibility for the change.

Reduce

We all wrestle with various fears. Two of these are a fear of change and a fear of rejection. The fear of change, its difficulty

The fear of rejection may be most frightening for a Christian.

and consequences, can be reduced. We have said that change is inevitable—but it can still be quite scary. That is how the unknown effects most of us. Try to remember that each small step forward needs to be met with your genuine encouragement and praise.

Yet, it is the fear of rejection that may be most frightening for a Christian. Satan continually seeks to sow seeds of judgment and criticism within the church. Unfortunately, some Christians fall into this paralyzing habit. Consider how you may respond if you are told something that shocks you. Perhaps something you wish you did not know. What will you say about admitted sin? I recall my response to a Christian man who confessed his adultery to me. I said, "You knew I would be up front with you about the sin of adultery when you came to see me.

When you begin your feedback with compliments and a few words of encouragement, the Enemy's plan is defeated.

Yet, I am impressed by your openness and honesty. I can see that you are now struggling with a difficult transition, whether to go forward with God and rebuild your marriage, or to continue living with lies and possibly losing your marriage.

"I also think it took a great deal of courage to come and talk to me in the first place. It shows that this is an issue that you are very serious about. You clearly have the determination to follow through once you make a decision. The question before you is which direction is your life going to go. Are you going to go forward with God, or continue in your direction away from Him? This is a question you will need to answer."

I believe we have liberty to "normalize" the experience of sin—after all, we all have sinned. None of us can "cast the first stone." Only God can cast it at those we seek to help, and He is completely committed to their success—and has provided a means for them to achieve it. Therefore, when you begin your "feedback" with compliments and a few words of encouragement, the Enemy's plan is defeated. Instead of receiving your criticism, they have received their first clear ray of hope.

Review

At this point, for those who were able to envision new possibilities, it is advisable to review what their "moving picture" looked like. (For those persons who were not able to proceed "through a doorway," there is, of course, no review. Just finish with a simple task. More on the task later.) When we review it we reinforce it. Instead of reinforcing their problem, which they have already been doing quite successfully, you are now taking a moment to reinforce their image of a solution. Again, this is a brief review, simply describing what they will be doing instead, or what they will be doing specifically. How will they be doing it. What they will be doing differently. How they will know that they're on track.

For example, with parents who were going to try to help their son feel more loved, I helped them summarize and rehearse their goal in this way: "You said that you usually showed your love by providing for his physical needs and you both felt that this should be enough, but now you have discovered that it hasn't been. Since what you have been doing has not been working quite like you hoped it would, you have decided to try doing something different. You mentioned that you would no longer assume that he knows you love him. Instead you will specifically go out of your way to tell him, while finding the time to get out alone with him individually. You also said you will now seek to make loving eye contact as often as possible, to touch and hug him often each day."

They need to create many new loving memories if they wish to replace or alter older, more hurtful ones.

In this way the start of a potential solution is being clearly described and acknowledged one more time before the conversation ends. Of course this has not "fixed" any deep-rooted issues. That is not the intention of supportive counseling. Our purpose is to simply support the Holy Spirit and to trust His intention. Helping them get unstuck and back on track is a wonderful way to allow God's Spirit to begin their healing. They need to create many new loving memories if they wish to replace or alter their older, more hurtful ones. It stands to reason that the actions they take today will be the memories they enjoy tomorrow.

Remember that we want this solution to come out of their lives and experiences. This will occur as a simple result of asking questions that focus on solutions, clarifying that focus, and then doing a small part of what has been imagined to observe what happens. This last part is called presenting a simple task.

Task

After you have offered encouragement for any noticed effort, sought to reduce fears, and, for those who went through a doorway, reviewed the potential solution, it is now time to draw the conversation to a close. Your final words will be to offer a specific suggestion or task. Unlike suggestions that flow from advice that seems good to the giver, this suggestion will only reinforce the imagined solution. As we have said earlier, it is easier to act your way into a feeling than to feel your way into an action. Remember what Will Rogers said: "Even if you are on the right track, you'll get run over if you just sit there."

Thus the task will invite the deliberate thinking and living of a part of the solution. Its purpose is to encourage a kind of ripple effect, like the ripples on a pond. These ripples are the new interactions that are the result of "doing" a bit of the imagined solution. What one person does affects the next person, who then reacts differently, which affects the next, and so forth. As King Solomon advised us, we should cast our bread upon the waters and after a while we will find it again (Eccl. 11:1). Our hope is that those we are helping will continue to experience some positive changes long after they have left our presence. Again, they are doing the real work as they come into agreement with the Holy Spirit.

As I mentioned earlier, if none of the doorways are helpful, this does not imply that your time with this person has been a failure. They have been heard—which alone, is an act of love. It simply means that the shift in thinking—from problems to potential solutions—was not achieved. A task needs to be given with this in mind. Thus, *a simple task would help them to consider or observe something in the days ahead that may lead toward a solution.* Ask them to observe what happens in their (life, marriage, family, job, and so forth) this week that they want to continue to have happen. The key is that they specifically look for and take note of such things, no matter how seemingly insignificant. Then, the next time you talk you could ask them about these observations and hopefully see them proceed through a doorway, following once again the supportive counseling diagram.

For those with whom you have been able to review a potential solution, the task would be to have them do a portion of what you have reviewed. As I explained in chapter 2, there are four uncomplicated steps to this suggestion:

1. Do a small piece of the envisioned solution.
2. Carefully look for what works when you do it.
3. Deliberately do more of what worked.
4. Always observe what takes place when you do so.

For example, a couple who was at a three on a scale of one to ten was able to describe what will be different when they are at a four or a five. The simple task was offered in these words: "What I would like you to try this week is to deliberately do whatever it takes to move up to a four or a five on the scale we were talking about. It will probably be a part of what you have already described. When you do, I want you to take notice of what is helping. You don't need to write anything down, just make a mental note. Whatever you do to move along the track that is helping, I would like you to intentionally do some more of it.

"Again, please take note of what happens that is different when you do this. Just ask yourselves what is different within you emotionally, and what do you notice that is different with your spouse or your family. I think it would also be helpful to continue to let each other know what is working so you can work together to do more of it on purpose." In this way they will reinforce what they have noticed—both to themselves and to one another. Also, the Holy Spirit will better guide them into a lifestyle that is more fulfilling to them and more pleasing to Him.

FINAL THOUGHTS

I am sure you noticed that the supportive counsel diagram is a continuing circle. The reason is that any further counseling conversations with the persons you have been helping will follow the same basic processes. Again, always hear what their experience has been with the task that was given, and once invited in, proceed to an appropriate doorway in response to their present condition. For example, if no improvement was noticed, you may want to proceed directly to the inside doorway. Always assume God's activity and preparation. I encourage you to keep all supportive counseling very short term—one or two conversations. Please *do not* maintain long-term counseling relationships unless you are specifically gifted and trained to do so. *Do* maintain gracious Christian fellowship and affirm the continuing love and support of the family of God. Always remember to refer when your support is no longer helping. You are not going to be able to assist every type of person. God is the only perfect counselor.

If you feel drawn to know more about helping others, I recommend my textbook *Solution-Focused Pastoral Counseling* (Zondervan). Please feel free to contact me via e-mail at cakollar@erols.com if you have any questions, or if you require any information regarding training opportunities.

In closing, always be ready to encourage, love, and support to the very best of your ability all who are on the ride of life. Each soul is unique and priceless. In so doing you will be affirming your own place in God's design as you continue in the process of mastering life. More important, you will be showing yourself as a true servant of life's only true Master . . . Jesus.

THE BORING FIGURE

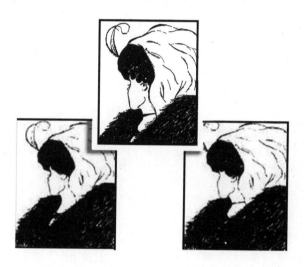

The top illustration is the original. The one on the left reveals the young woman with her head turned toward her right shoulder. The illustration on the right shows the old hag with her chin pointing toward the lower left corner of the picture.

Change Your Focus and Change Lives Faster

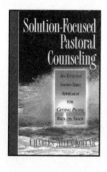

Solution-Focused Pastoral Counseling
An Effective Short-Term Approach for Getting People Back on Track
Charles Allen Kollar

Discover a fresh, effective, and time-saving approach to pastoral counseling.

Solution-Focused Pastoral Counseling shifts the emphasis from the problem to the strengths, vision, and practical solutions that lie within the individual. Dr. Kollar first lays the theological and theoretical groundwork for short-term counseling, then shows you how to ably apply the theory to sessions that help people get back on track.

Hardcover: ISBN 0-310-21346-0

ZondervanPublishingHouse
Grand Rapids, Michigan 49530
http://www.zondervan.com

A Division of HarperCollins*Publishers*

We want to hear from you. Please send your comments about this
book to us in care of the address below. Thank you.

ZondervanPublishingHouse
Grand Rapids, Michigan 49530
http://www.zondervan.com